THE

EVERYTHING

BABY SHOWER BOOK

From surprise parties to office
celebrations, how to throw an
outstanding event for the mother-to-be

Jennifer Jenkins

Adams Media Corporation
Holbrook, Massachusetts

An Everything® Series Book.
Everything® is a registered trademark of Adams Media Corporation.

Published by Adams Media Corporation
260 Center Street, Holbrook, MA 02343. U.S.A.

ISBN: 1-58062-305-0

Printed in the United States of America.

J I H G F E D C B

Library of Congress Cataloging-in-Publication Data

Jenkins, Jennifer
The everything baby shower book / Jennifer Jenkins.
p. cm.
Includes index.
ISBN 1-58062-305-0
1. Showers (Parties). I. Title.
GV1472.7.S5 J45   2000
                              99-056502

This publication is designed to provide accurate and authoritative information with
regard to the subject matter covered. It is sold with the understanding that the publisher
is not engaged in rendering legal, accounting, or other professional advice. If legal
advice or other expert assistance is required, the services of a competent professional
person should be sought.
— From a *Declaration of Principles* jointly adopted by a Committee of the
American Bar Association and a Committee of Publishers and Associations

Illustrations by Barry Littmann and Kathie Kelleher.

*This book is available at quantity discounts for bulk purchases.
For information, call 1-800-872-5627.*

Visit our home page at http://www.adamsmedia.com

Contents

Chapter 1   Baby Shower Basics 1

Chapter 2   Special Issues for Special Parties 23

Chapter 3   Shower Themes 31

Chapter 4 🧸 How to Budget the Shower ... 109

Chapter 5 🧸 Choosing a Venue 115

Chapter 6 🧸 The Guest List 121

Chapter 7 🧸 Ringing the Dinner Bell 135

Chapter 8   Decorating Your Party 155

Chapter 9   Women Bearing Gifts 177

Chapter 10   Seamless Party
Management 101 181

Chapter 11   Great Shower Activities 197

Chapter 12   Party Favors 217

Chapter 13   Worksheets 227

Introduction

Oooh! Your friend is having a baby! Whether it's her first or fifth, it's good cause for celebration! And you are the dear sweet friend (or sister or coworker) who has decided to host the shower for her. What fun you're about to have!

For your friend, preparing to have a baby is a time-consuming task. From frequent doctor appointments to learning about labor and delivery and breathing right to deciding what color to paint the nursery, new parents-to-be can get worn out! Now is a great time for a party! Usually hosted by a best girlfriend or the grandma-to-be, the baby shower is a chance for everyone to wish the new Mommy well, and buy all those cute little baby things.

If you're the one who wants to host the baby shower, buying a gift is the easy part. Hosting the shower requires a bit more effort. What you need is help, and this is it. From the tightest budget to the most lavish bank account, this is the *complete* guide to baby showers. It will help you pull off a flawless party that will be a dear memory for your friend, the other guests, and even for you for years to come.

We'll walk together step-by-step, based on your budget, your lifestyle, the mommy-to-be and your own desires. You'll learn exactly how to create the perfect baby shower, tailored to your wants and time constraints.

You'll find everything you need here. I've stuffed in all sorts of handy checklists—whether it's questions to ask the caterer or a shopping list for the grocery store. You'll find some premade sample parties, some clever hors d'oeuvres recipes, and even a few sample cake-decorating ideas. We'll talk about everything from a countdown for the arrangements to how much cake the average person eats at a party to what colors to use in decorating the location.

If you are a mother yourself, I'm sure you remember your own baby shower and what fun it was. If you haven't had babies, let me assure you the shower is one of the most joyful events of the last trimester of pregnancy! (And you thought it must be bloated legs, hating all your maternity clothes, and having total strangers tell you gory delivery stories in the grocery store!)

A baby shower celebrates the expected birth of a new child. In the old days, it was a celebration of the new life about to begin. But it was also a chance to get more baby clothes than you could possibly hand-sew yourself in nine months, what with needing to bale the hay, milk the cows, weed the vegetable garden, and wash clothes in the stream along with all your other tasks.

Today, a baby shower still represents the joy of friends and family as they await the birth of a new child. A new baby represents the potential of a fresh life to all of us. It represents the cycle of life; it's an event of hope and joy. When I had my third child, my mother gave me a lovely picture that said, "A Baby Is God's Way of Saying the World Should Go On."

This baby shower can be an event your friends will always remember, and since you're going to do it right—and do it with style—it's an event you'll always remember with happiness, too. Like anything else in life, if you follow the directions, things are definitely easier.

You'll be glad you found such a complete and thorough companion, and your friends will rave about your success. You might just find yourself being hired to throw showers for friends of friends in the future!

So here's a toast to the mommy-to-be, to the new baby, and to you, for the kindness you're showing by deciding to host her baby shower. Here's to a great time had by all, and a safe delivery, and a happy life for the new little one about to join us.

CHAPTER 1

Baby Shower Basics

Who Wears the Diapers? . . . Oops! I Mean Pants

If you're the one who is pulling off this whole thing, you get to decide exactly how the shower will go. You get to decide if you'll try to surprise her, or if you will simply send her an invitation along with the rest of the guests. Will you have it outdoors in the sunshine and flowers, or in someone's house? Whatever you choose, whatever you do, whether your shower is at a country club or in your living room, it's something your expectant friend will remember for the rest of her life with gratitude and warmth.

There are many decisions to be made as you prepare for the shower. This can be fun, or it can stress you out. A lot of it depends on you. Follow along in the book, and we'll make it fun together. Basically, planning a shower (or any other party) comes down to five basic things.

The 5 Ws of Baby Shower Planning

Hosting a baby shower doesn't have to be a lot of work, and it doesn't have to cost a lot of money. This book will help you make the shower something to remember whether or not you have a large budget. I'll give you simple step-by-step guidance for everything from how to invite people to how to entertain your guests to when to send them all home. You'll get help with *everything* you can think of here. Basically, you've bought the right book. (It's not like you purchased that other book sitting beside this one at the bookstore— the *A Few of the Things You Need To Know About Planning a Perfect Baby Shower.*) So we come to the basics. These are all simply a matter of logic. Here are the almost 5 Ws involved in baby shower planning. They are:

- Who will you invite?
- What will you do during it?
- How much can you spend (time and/or money)?
- Where will you have it?
- When will you have it?

What If a Bunch of People Will Want to Throw Her a Shower?

To rattle your security even further, I have to warn you you may not be the only person who is even thinking about throwing her a shower. What about that? What if someone has already beaten you to the punch (bowl)? Hmmm.

What with work friends and friends from the mommy-to-be's club, church, school, old family friends, or any one of many disparate groups in a woman's life, chances are there will be plenty of people who want to throw her a baby shower. Probably lots of them don't even know one another. Who's the right one to do it, and how many showers can she have?

That question is answered in many ways. The issue is primarily the comfort of the guests. It is redundant and possibly a financial drain on anyone to be invited to more than two showers for the same woman. With that in mind, it can also make a shower a lot more fun for the new mom if groups of people she knows from different parts of her world can meet. Her best friend at work can finally meet Aunt Mabel, about whom she has heard so many stories. It's a kick for some women to watch this, and babies soften everyone's hearts. It's a very family, nurturing sort of time anyway. On the other hand, co-workers might not feel generally comfortable at the family get-together, or members outside the mother-to-be's religious community may be uncomfortable if fervent believers surround them. Mixing different groups from her life might establish more intimacy with the mother-to-be than she feels comfortable with.

There's also the ability to share the expenses and work of the party if you cohost with other people from different areas of her life. You might find you enjoy working closely with her best friend from work or church to cohost something with her and your friend's group of friends from that organization.

A Tradition of Celebrating

Women in nearly all cultures have a tradition for celebrating the mother-to-be and soon-to-be born baby. In the Navajo Native American tradition, the mother-to-be is sung over in a ceremony performed especially for expectant mothers. In Navajo it is called "dine bizzaad," which is usually translated as the Blessingway. The purpose of the tradition is to bring about a harmonious, successful entry into the world. The songs sung invoke all that is good and favorable and oppose all that is evil.

On the first night near the time the birth is expected, the mother-to-be is sung over with a few songs. The next day she has a ritual bath with songs and prayers. That evening there is an all night sing for her and her baby-to-be.

But what if the mother-to-be wouldn't like that? As the hostess of the party, the easiest way to resolve this is to ask the daddy-to-be what he believes she'd want, if you don't know yourself. As long as one or two poor souls don't get invited to more than two showers for the same new mom, everything will work out just fine. Some of her friends might make new friends with other people who are important in her life.

These factors should be reasonably considered before you proceed. In our disassociated world, lots of times a person has three or four social groups to which they belong, and they never really overlap. If your expectant friend is an extrovert and you don't mind doing some sleuthing to get all the names and addresses to send invitations, mingling groups in her life might make the party even more wonderful. Once you are certain this is what you want to do, and that you won't be offending any other group of people by holding a shower for her, you're ready to go on to the next most important question:

Can You Keep a Secret?

Surprise baby showers are probably the most fun. The expectant mother knows that most likely, her friends *will* have a shower for her, but she isn't sure when. I've known women to cry that they were unloved and no one was going to throw them a shower up until the moment they walked into the room and saw the assembled partygoers!

I believe that if you can pull it off, a surprise shower is far and away the most fun. If you will be inviting men, it might be slightly harder to keep the shower secret, depending on your social rules. No offense, but not having been raised socially with the idea of secret baby showers, every time a surprise shower I know of has been spoiled, it's been spoiled by a guy apologizing to the guest of honor for not being able to attend . . . in advance.

If you are going to make this a surprise shower, first you have to figure out when the mom-to-be is available. Ask her husband or even her mother to figure it out if you don't know her schedule. (Which, by the way, will be in a state of flux right before the

Pregnancy Myopia

When I was pregnant with my third child, the last thing I expected was a baby shower. Having had a boy and a girl I was sure no one would think I needed any more pink or blue baby clothes, or any other gadgets or baby paraphernalia.

My friend Sharon had two small girls, Mandy and Lauren. They were into playing with dolls, so when I walked into their home and saw a bassinet in the living room, I thought nothing of it. I assumed it was for the girls' dolls. We sat down on her couch and chatted for about ten minutes. I was very narcissistic about my coming baby and totally focused on that impending event, and not on any other point of interest in Sharon's house. I'd been there so many times I didn't look to see new things anymore. There were plenty of clues I should have picked up on.

I can scarcely express my surprise when we walked into her backyard ten minutes later to "see her new rose bushes," and the yard was full of perhaps twenty families who'd all come to celebrate my coming baby! They'd kept so quiet! I'd been so oblivious. So it's possible to have a surprise party. It's even probable. I think that for myself and the women I've known, the last trimester finds them very focused on their coming baby (often called "nesting behavior" in the pregnancy books) and not on external circumstances.

shower, no doubt. Incumbent babies have a way of needing an awful lot of things done to prepare for their entry into the world!)

Once you have a few possible dates, share them with your cohosts at the planning meeting (mentioned later) or choose one yourself. When selecting a date (more on this later, too), remember that some of the people you will want to invite won't be able to make it. That's life. Too bad for them. As Lincoln said, "You can please some of the people some of the time, but you cannot please all of the people all of the time." Do the best you can, but don't make yourself crazy by trying to choose a time when everyone is going to be available.

For a surprise party, you will need an accomplice to bring her to the shower. This could be a coworker, her husband, her mother, or another friend. It cannot be someone with whom she doesn't usually spend social time, because that's too obvious. If a friend calls her from out of the blue and says, "I want to spend time with you before the baby is born. Would 7 P.M. on Tuesday, November 11, work?" it is going to be a dead giveaway, especially if it's July.

The showers where I have successfully pulled off a surprise followed a pretty simple formula: Make a plan; change the plan at "the last minute" to throw her off the scent, as they say; set it for another time that you knew in advance she'd be free; and then hold the shower. In other words, select a date now. Using your accomplice, who knows her schedule, set it up for, say, November 6 (assuming it's late September when you call and you already know she's free then!). Then, on November 1, when she absolutely knows that you are going to be taking her to the baby shower but she hasn't said anything, call and change it. Something came up. Can you do it on the 11th instead? That definitely will surprise her, unless someone screws it up. And if someone does, oh well. It isn't the end of the world.

Now that you have the tricks down, how do you keep other guests from spoiling the fun? On the invitation, write in big RED LETTERS "Ssssh! Surprise Party! If you accidentally tell her, survivors will be prosecuted to the fullest extent of the law!" (Or something equally silly, but that kind of warning makes it really stick in people's minds. Trust me. This is the voice of experience.)

Other than that, short of not bumping into her at the party goods store with your arms full of little pink and blue plastic booties, there's not a whole lot to spoil the surprise. There's even more about surprise showers in Chapter 3.

Setting a Date and Checking It Twice

Make sure you select a date the mom-to-be has free and one that her husband assures you he will help her keep clear. Ideally, the mother-to-be or her spouse will be able to give you several dates that would work in her last trimester. (A trimester is three months.) In this case, a shower is typically sometime in the three months before the baby is due. There are special timing notes in the sections on sorority, office, and church showers about selecting the ideal time/date. Most showers occur about six to eight weeks before the birth/delivery date, not often more, but sometimes less.

Time to Party!

We've talked about setting a date, so now we need to discuss setting a time. Depending on the vitality level of your expectant friend, you might want to schedule the party in the afternoon, early evening, night, or weekend. There are some considerations extant in all of them.

If you do it during the day on a weekday, women who work will likely not be able to attend, but it could be more relaxing, especially if you/she/many of the women have school-age kids who will be otherwise occupied at that time of day. Many kids are in school until 3 P.M., so you could do it earlier than that and avoid the pandemonium of all the kids at your house.

If you do it in the early evening during the work week, those who have to commute will perhaps have to deal with traffic, which could blow their being there for the big "Surprise!" moment. But your friend might find she has more energy in the early evening. (Remember, how she feels in the fourth month isn't how she will feel in the eighth in most cases!)

If you want the maximum number of people in attendance, or she belongs to a church with far-flung members who would all like to attend, you might want to do it on the weekend. This is the most common time for showers. That way, people have more time to commute, and it's often less of a problem. The challenge with weekend showers is that they are highly suspect to the mom-to-be. How many times in the last year has your shill asked her out, out of the blue, on a weekend?

How Many Hours Long Is a Typical Shower?

An evening dessert-and-coffee girls-only shower would probably last about three hours, but advertise it in the invitations as lasting only two. You'd want to start it late enough so everyone can get through traffic from work, eat dinner, and still make it end early enough so everyone can get up the next day for work again.

If you are planning a weekend shower, especially a coed one, the sky's the limit on time. Figure about five hours. Advertise four in your invitations.

If you're trying to answer this question for catering/room-rental purposes, use three hours as a rule of thumb. Two hours is how long it will officially last, and the third hour will be for happy hangers-on to chat with your mother-to-be and straggle out.

Money Makes the World Go Round: What Can You Spend?

The next most important question is How much money and time can you spend on this event? No other question will be more influential on your party, or more clearly influence what sort of party you will hold. Except if maybe you shouldn't be doing it at all.

Money is a direct factor of time. If you have more money than time, then you can have the perfect shower with very little time invested, because you can get others (catering companies, cake decorators, florists, etc.), to handle many of the party details for you. However, if you are like most people and you have more time than money, then you must not only work out how that time is best spent for maximum impact but also how you can get others to help you maximize the time you have to create a truly splendid party for your friend. If you use a little imagination and some of the tips I offer you in this book, you can create a truly memorable, wonderful party no matter what your budget. I'm going to show you how.

There are more ideas in this book than you could use if you threw twenty-five baby showers. All you have to do now is pick and choose your favorites so that you can create something that is uniquely you and your friends.

You can do a basic party in someone's home with twelve guests for about $150 or less. You can go nuts and spend a couple grand if you do it at a rented location with catering for fifty people. I'm going to guess you're going to land somewhere in the middle. Let's say about $250 max.

Party Angel Investors

Of course, there are clever ways to increase your budget if that last number of $250 made you feel weak-kneed. You can get money from other people who would like to cosponsor with you, or from others who will attend or would like to attend the shower. Why will these people give you money? Because they don't have the time/money/energy to host a shower themselves. You'll acknowledge them by including their names as cohosts in the invitations. It might be a nice gesture for people who want to be helpful but cannot be more active. Don't think of yourself as a pity case; think of it as offering others the chance to get involved. Here's a list of people who might like to contribute money to the expenses of this baby shower:

- The grandparents-to-be who cannot fly in for the shower
- Other relatives who can't be there
- Her mother or mother-in-law
- Her company or place of employment
- Her women's group or church group
- Her classmates or the girls in her aerobics class
- Friends who will attend but cannot take the time/afford to do it themselves
- Her out-of-state best friend who will be attending but can't be that useful in preparations

Guests as Photographers

Encourage guests to bring cameras. In fact it is suggested to have at least one camera for every seven guests. You might even buy some disposable cameras and pass them out as guests arrive. Make it clear you want to have many pictures of this event.

If you find guests are too caught up in gabbing and are forgetting to take pictures, designate a couple of people as evening photographers.

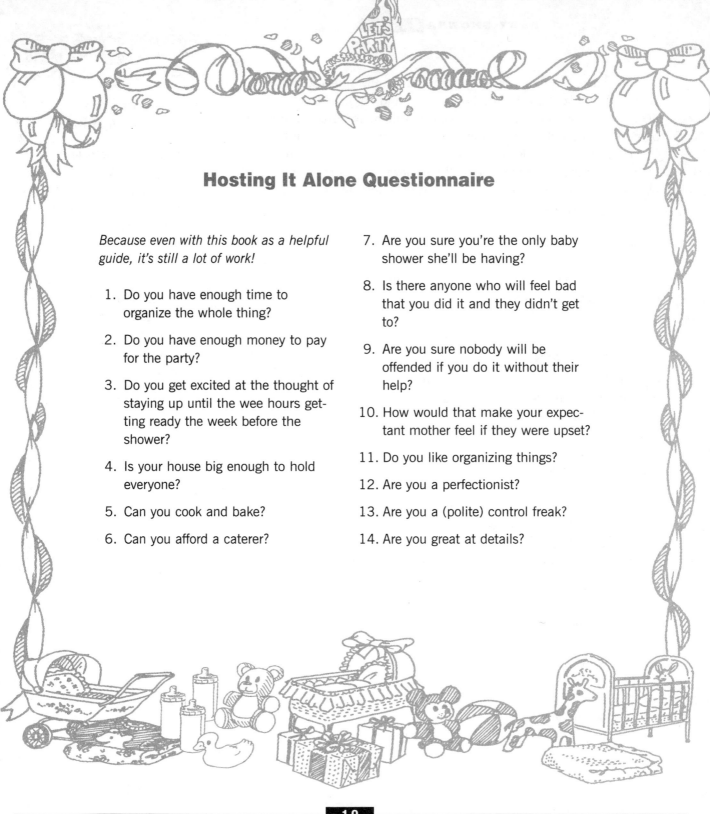

Hosting It Alone Questionnaire

Because even with this book as a helpful guide, it's still a lot of work!

1. Do you have enough time to organize the whole thing?

2. Do you have enough money to pay for the party?

3. Do you get excited at the thought of staying up until the wee hours getting ready the week before the shower?

4. Is your house big enough to hold everyone?

5. Can you cook and bake?

6. Can you afford a caterer?

7. Are you sure you're the only baby shower she'll be having?

8. Is there anyone who will feel bad that you did it and they didn't get to?

9. Are you sure nobody will be offended if you do it without their help?

10. How would that make your expectant mother feel if they were upset?

11. Do you like organizing things?

12. Are you a perfectionist?

13. Are you a (polite) control freak?

14. Are you great at details?

Of course, there are people you should not ask to contribute:
- Her
- Her husband
- Her obstetrician
- And some people would say, any member of her family (I don't agree)

Sister, Can You Spare a Dime?

If you're going to pay for the shower yourself, I'm sure you are skipping this section. But it actually is a nice thing for you to ask people to be involved in paying for the shower, and any other level of participation they'd like. You get two benefits: shared responsibilities and shared expenses. It can only make your life easier. But you must ask appropriately, so those who cannot afford to help don't feel sad or embarrassed. Here's my suggestion, taken from my literary agent, Wendy Keller. She has spent her whole career asking people for money for things that don't exist yet. Wendy says to ask them but leave them an out. Try something like this: "You know, Martha, I'm thinking about hosting Debbie's baby shower. I can do a basic shower myself, but it feels like it would be great if we could do something really special for Debbie. Do you know anyone who might like to contribute a few dollars to help me make this shower really incredible?"

Be prepared to answer the question, "How much is a few dollars?" Here's what to say. "Well, Martha, I'm thinking I'd like to invite all the women of Debbie's family as well as her friends from church and work. That's about thirty-five women. I figure it will cost about $200 for the basic shower, and I could use maybe $50/$100 more for something really fabulous. Of course, whoever helps me will be listed on the invitations as the cohost. Do you know anyone who'd like to cohost with me?"

You've given Martha an out by asking if she knows anyone, not asking her directly if she will give you money. You've tried to close her twice. ("Close" is a sales term for asking for the sale.) You've baited her by offering the idea of all the fabulous things that will happen if she/someone else contributes. You've given the personal payback—a fabulous party with her/someone else as cohost.

If she doesn't bite, try the next name on your list. According to my agent, another sales adage is, "Maybe means Yes, and No means

Maybe." It's just a matter of finding the right trigger for someone, assuming they have the money/time/inclination to contribute.

If Martha says no, that she cannot help, or no, she doesn't know anyone, you can say, "Do you want to help me prepare for the party?" If she says yes, you can assign her a task from the delegation list found later in this book. See? That's pretty easy! Tell her you'll get in touch with her in a few days/weeks when you know what you'd like her to do.

Not only is it easy, but if you're feeling guilty about wanting to ask for help, remember that you are giving them a chance to give to someone they care about, too. If they were hosting the party and had to hire an expert baby shower party planner (which you will be by the time you close this book!), they'd pay a lot of money to get your services.

But before you call potential contributors, you need to ask yourself . . .

Do You Want to Do It All Alone? Money versus Authority Considerations

Let's just assume you want to host the party all by yourself, for whatever reason. You don't care how much work it is, you don't care how much money it costs, you don't care that your house will be trashed after fifteen women leave the party. You just plain want to do it all alone. You're a control freak like me, for instance.

OK. You can do it all by yourself, and with all the work will come all the glory and the mommy-to-be's undying thanks. Cool. But please, consider the questions in the box before you absolutely make up your mind.

If you can honestly say yes to most of these questions, you should definitely do it yourself. But there are some benefits to having other people involved:

- Sharing the expenses
- Tapping into someone else's creativity
- Providing a great place to have the shower if they have a bigger house

✂ Cutting down on the amount of time all this will take you

✂ Making your life a lot easier while still giving a great party

✂ Including people you like who cannot or would not do it themselves

✂ Giving yourself more time to conduct your regular life outside of the shower the two weeks before you do it.

So will you cohost it with someone else? Will you allow other people to invest but handle all the details yourself? Or will you do this all yourself?

Ha-ha! You didn't even notice, but you've already gotten through TWO of the 5 Ws of shower planning. Was that easy or what? You're a star!

If You've Decided to Cohost the Shower, Here Are Some Tips

Cohosting offers lots of benefits, not the least of which are shared expenses and shared responsibilities. You might become great friends (if you aren't already) with whomever you cohost the shower. You could also want to kill each other and that tension could mess up the party.

Luckily, you bought this book. Here is the secret to cohosting a fabulous party and having fun doing it. Get ready to commit the secret to memory:

Decide who will do what now,
while it's all still a fun theory.

The more you work out now, the easier this whole thing will be for you. (It's kind of like a prenuptial agreement before a wedding. Nobody really wants to think about What If . . . but What If happens sometimes.)

So you've gotten a partner or two together. The first step is to have a planning meeting with your partner(s). You will want to buy a copy of this book for each of them (my publisher told me to put that in, but it's a good idea), and you will want to copy (and enlarge) the "Delegation Chart/To Do List."

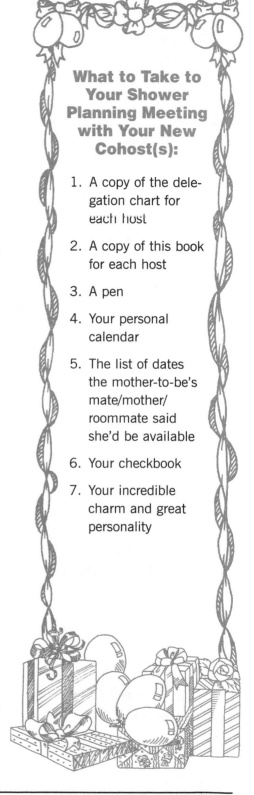

What to Take to Your Shower Planning Meeting with Your New Cohost(s):

1. A copy of the delegation chart for each host

2. A copy of this book for each host

3. A pen

4. Your personal calendar

5. The list of dates the mother-to-be's mate/mother/roommate said she'd be available

6. Your checkbook

7. Your incredible charm and great personality

The following form should be filled out and one copy given to each cohost.

Party For

To be held on: ....

Where: ....

From what time to what time: ....

Names/phone numbers/e-mails of cohosts: ....

....

Theme: (choose one from this book or come up with something of your own!)

....

....

Invitations:

Choosing or making them ....

Buying ....

Writing ....

Drawing a map ....

Mailing ....

Handling RSVPs ....

Party Decorations:

Selecting ....

Buying ....

Storing ....

Assembling ....

Hanging/Decorating ....

Removing ....

Menu:

Choosing the menu

Buying food

Baking/buying cake

Making food

Setting up food

Serving food

Cleaning up kitchen

Location Rental and Setup:

Selecting a location

Renting a location

Paying the deposit

Preparing a house

Paying for the rental space

Setting up the furniture

Renting the furniture

Returning any rented furniture

Cleaning the house afterward

Removing debris from the rental space/house

Getting back any deposit

Party Favors:

Choosing party favors

Buying various favors or their components

Making party favors

Assembling party favors

Distributing party favors

Party Games:

Choosing which games to play

Choosing an entertainer

Paying for an entertainer

Assembling anything necessary

Finding prizes

Buying prizes

Organizing the games

Emceeing the games

Managing the games

Judging the games

Removing or taking down the games

Music:

Choosing the type of music

Engaging a musician

Paying a musician

Providing CDs or other recordings

Making sure the stereo works well

Changing the music during the party

Making sure the CDs go back to whomever owns them

The Gift Table:

Renting or allocating a gift table

Decorating a gift table

Welcoming and taking gifts from attendees at the door

Making sure cards stay with attendees' gifts

Recording who gave the mom-to-be what

Packing all her gifts into big boxes

Putting the big boxes in her trunk

Cleaning up the wrapping paper and ribbons

Assembling the ribbon bouquet for the baby's room

Your job at this first meeting with your cohost(s) is basically to decide on a date, a time, and a theme and get a general idea of who will do what and how you'll pay for it all. You probably want to have the first meeting with your cohost(s) face to face if at all possible. You will have called the mother-to-be's husband (or her) already and determined you are the only friends who will be throwing the shower, and gotten a couple of possible dates and times she's available. Or, if it's not a surprise, you will have asked her directly.

Existentialism and Baby Showers: Who Am I?

It's OK if you don't know your cohost(s). Take control of the meeting by showing her how prepared you are. Give her the book and the chart, and after you're done giggling and bonding over sugar and caffeine, choose the date, set a budget, and, ideally, select the location. (If you plan to rent a location, you won't be able to select a place at your first meeting, obviously, because you will have to check availability.) Then, decide on a theme.

Then, generally go over the list of things to be done. Make a verbal, out-loud deal in advance to be honest about what your real interests are. Don't sit there like a mouse if you love to bake and would love to make her cake, but you hate picking out music because all you listen to is Old Elvis and everyone teases you about it. Tell your cohost(s) you want to make the darn cake! Pick the jobs you like, letting her pick the jobs she likes, and negotiate the rest. Be clear about what you are interested in doing, and what you vehemently DON'T want to do. Chances are, you and your cohost(s) can sweet-talk somebody else into doing what neither of you wants to do, or you can pool your money and hire it done.

At this first meeting, you also want to talk about money. Who will pay for what is kind of taken care of in the delegation chart, but if you want to do a straight budget, refer to the budget-planning section of this book. A nice home party can be done for $250. From there, the sky's the limit. Reasonably elegant home parties for fifteen people would cost about $400, self-catered, but including the gift you guys give her. Lavish, well, you gotta do some price shopping yourself to discover that one. If you hire Dr. T. Berry Brazelton or Penelope Leach to come lecture you on parenting as a surprise guest, it's going to cost a lot more.

If You've Decided to Go It Alone . . .

Doing it all by your lonesome DOES NOT mean you cannot get all sorts of help with any part you want help with!

Let's say you want to do it alone, but you want a really cool location. Ask another friend, the mother-to-be's mom or somebody else to let you do it at their place. If you can sweet-talk a friend who has a great house and who would let you use his or her house or yard for the party, you've got a perfect deal!

Know this: The person whose house it is at is usually considered the hostess, no matter what the facts may be, unless the homeowner is a stranger to the attendees. Also, no matter where you are having it, you should psychologically prepare yourself for some breakage. Especially if alcohol will be served. Five percent of even the most perfect parties go wrong—and you just want to make it look like it's all flowing as planned. Never get ruffled, no matter what happens.

The Question is . . . . what do you want help with?

- Help with cooking? Do it potluck!
- Help with the cake? Ask one of the attendees who you know loves to bake to make it her shower gift.
- Help sending out and tracking the invitations? Ask someone with a computer, like a secretary friend who is also a friend of the mom-to-be's.
- Help with the party games? You certainly know someone in the group who is always the life of the party and who would love the job.
- Help tracking down party goods? Get someone who can afford the leisure time of strolling through a half dozen places on their days off.
- Help making the party favors? Ask a friend who's into crafts.

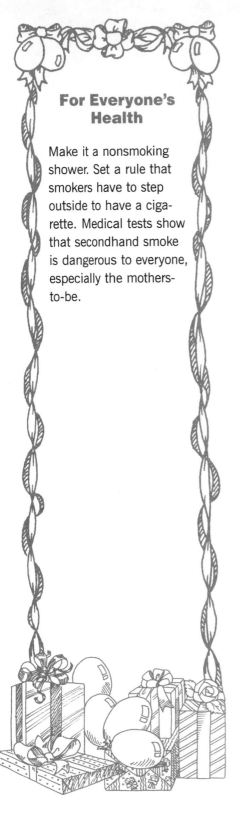

See? Doing it all by yourself doesn't mean doing it all by yourself. It means you get to practice your skills as a kind and effective manager of others.

Who Does What?

Ever Wonder What YOU Are Supposed to Do?

Have fun! After all this work, the party should unfurl close to perfectly! Make sure the food is hot or cold, the drinks don't get too diluted and no one gets too drunk to drive. Other than that, keep people fed and happy and everything will be a masterpiece. You may have discovered a new career option for yourself!

Does the Mother-to-Be Have Any Responsibilities?

First, before planning a shower, you should decide if it will be a surprise or not. If not, ask the mother-to-be if she wants you to have it for her. Surprise showers are not ideal for many people, and they can be a lot harder for you to plan. Further, the cat sometimes gets out of the bag by accident anyway.

If you ask the mother-to-be and she says yes, then she is reasonably expected to do the following: She should provide you with a guest list that roughly matches the number of people you want to have. (This means you have to tell her in advance—the average number for a home shower is fifteen.) She should give you about fifteen to twenty names, because not everyone will be able to make it. It's kind of her responsibility to make sure no one she knows is invited to more than two showers, which gets to be a drag for the poor guest. She should also be pretty much OK with the type of shower you want to throw. Unless it's way outside her comfort zone, this should be no problem. And she needs to tell you the names/locations of the store(s) where she's registered for baby gifts, if applicable.

Does the Mother-to-Be Have Any Responsibilities after the Shower?

A long time ago, she was expected to personally write thank-you notes to each person who attended and gave a gift. But Emily Post has been gone a long time. Now it's fine for her to just thank the people who are there, and probably write a brief thank-you to people who couldn't attend but sent a gift anyway.

Also, gosh, a real pal might choose to stay and help you clean up a little, but she's got so many other responsibilities right now that even if she offers you'll probably urge her to go home and get some sleep. Growing a baby takes effort! She's probably exhausted. Besides, that's why you budgeted for one day's maid service tomorrow.

CHAPTER 2

Special Issues for Special Parties

Am I Nuts for Doing This Shower?

There could be a moment or two in the next few weeks while you are planning this shower when you think, "Gee, why am I doing this anyway?" Especially if you have never been a mother-to-be and had your own shower, if you have small children, if you work full time, if you have anything else to do all day other than plan parties.

You are planning this party because you want everyone to have a memorable time, or a fun time, or for her to know how much you care about her, or because she is your dear colleague. Or are you also hoping to make new friends? To practice your organizational skills? How about because you wonder if you would like to quit your day job and become a caterer or party planner for a living?

Once you know *why* you want to host this party, you need to think about the kind of person *you* are and the kind of person *she* is.

Measure Twice, Cut Once

If you and the mother-to-be are friends but your personality styles really don't match, you'll probably want to defer to *her* style as much as possible. After all, this party is for her.

Another important consideration is any physical limitations she might be having by the time the party rolls around. Let me assure you that walking up a steep staircase or climbing a short hill to reach a scenic mountain lookout is less than fun for most women in their last trimester.

Making Her Comfortable

If you haven't had a baby, imagine this:

- Women's joints soften to allow the pelvis to spread so the baby can get through the birth canal. This means long sitting on hard surfaces can be unpleasant. Provide a soft chair for your expectant mother. Don't make her sit outside on aluminum picnic benches for hours.

- The excessive pressure of a 6-or 7- pounds fetus on the bladder requires you to hold the shower at a place that has adequate bathroom facilities.
- Most women do not drink alcohol during their pregnancies. Plan on some nonalcoholic beverages.
- Most concerned modern mothers avidly avoid cigarette smoke when they are pregnant. Make sure you and your guests choose a place and behaviors that are considerate of your friend's unborn baby's health.
- Babies in utero tend to become disruptive kickers when exposed to loud rock music. Think about the expectant woman's personality style before you plan to take her dancing for the shower.
- Feet and ankles are often swollen by the end of the day, especially for women who have sit-down jobs. Don't have a party without seating, or one that requires a lot of walking.
- For multiparas (women who already have had at least one baby), the cervix can dilate long before labor actually begins, making them feel like they are splitting open on the inside. It's a rather achy feeling. Again, make the mom-to-be comfortable during the party by providing adequate seating.
- She might deliver early or, heaven forbid, have complications that blow your plans. Be prepared to be gracious, or possibly to switch your party location to the hospital room or elsewhere after the birth, depending on circumstances.
- Being pregnant increases the blood flow in a woman's body. That's why pregnant women suffer more in the heat than nonpregnant ones. Before you plan a garden or outdoor party, ask yourself how hot it will likely get on that day?
- Women carrying twins tend to deliver earlier—have the party plenty in advance—like in the mom-to-be's sixth month.
- Spicy food upsets some pregnant women. Make sure you have a range of foods if you are providing a meal.

I'm making it sound like pregnant women are fragile, but in reality how fragile any woman is when pregnant depends on a hundred health and vitality factors. If you know your friend well,

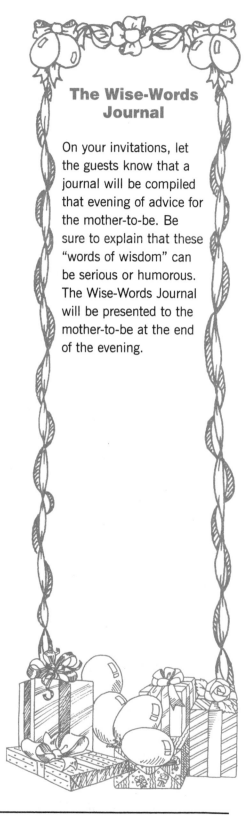

The Wise-Words Journal

On your invitations, let the guests know that a journal will be compiled that evening of advice for the mother-to-be. Be sure to explain that these "words of wisdom" can be serious or humorous. The Wise-Words Journal will be presented to the mother-to-be at the end of the evening.

assume she'll be only slightly more physically needy by the time the shower actually rolls around.

Of course, if she's leading prego-robics at the local gym, and looks like a stick figure with a fat belly, she might adore a baby shower spent with her husband at a local dance club, dinner theater, et cetera.

The thing to remember is this: This party should make her feel comfortable and happy. It should not embarrass her or bore her. The idea is a fun time out with a bunch of her friends—not a trip to the Outer Limits of her Comfort Zone.

What If We Cannot Have It Before the Birth?

If baby decides to show up early, or there are (heaven forbid!) complications that prevent her from attending her own shower before the birth, there's absolutely no reason you cannot have it afterward.

Special Notes for Coworker Showers

The ideal time to have a coworker shower is on one of the last days the new Mommy will be at work before her maternity leave begins. Who knows? The little darling may so beguile her she doesn't come back to work at all! Typically, colleagues gather together, often on lunch hour or right after work, and chow down on refreshments (cake, cookies, fruit, tea, soft drinks) and present a group gift.

Special Notes for Church Showers

If you're having a shower for a woman of your congregation, you probably know most of her friends. Unless her other friends and family are of the same faith, though, you might want to reconsider inviting "outsiders," especially if you will be holding it at the church or using any sort of religious rituals during the party. Run it past her husband before you make any final decisions, or check in with her if it's not a surprise shower.

Not that you need to be reminded, but some religious groups have particular jargon that could make a few outsiders feel uncomfortable. Think about this and discuss it with your new mom. This is NOT the time for making new converts.

If it is customary to pray before each meal in your faith, and the shower is being held in private, please go right ahead. But if it is customary and you are meeting in a public place for the shower, you simply must ask the new mom how she will feel about praying in public before you choose to do so. Her choice must be honored. If God/your Deity is blessing this birth, surely He/it will bless you for your love for and consideration of your spiritual sister's emotional comfort.

Special Notes for Club or Sorority Showers

Inviting the other women in your club or group is a given, but please ask the expectant woman's husband if he knows of any other baby showers before the baby is born. If there are not going to be, you have a social responsibility to invite the new mom's female family members, and probably also her friends from elsewhere, like work or church.

TWINS! Yikes!

Multiple live births are increasingly common in society today, thanks to the prevalence of fertility methods. If your friend is expecting more than one, be sure to inform potential guests who may not know they need to buy two (or three!) of everything they bring.

For Adopted Babies

Most new parents of adopted babies seem to prefer holding the shower AFTER their adoption is complete. Now everyone knows whether to get pink or blue. What a wonderful opportunity for friends to celebrate the blessing of this new little life for which their friends have taken responsibility.

Second—Third—Fourth or More Baby—Can We Still Give Her a Shower?

Why not? Go right ahead—she'll be even more surprised! If she's expecting a baby of the opposite gender, or if this is a midlife baby, or a "surprise baby," there's going to be little she'll appreciate more than another baby shower. So much the better if you're the one who threw the shower for her first baby! If she had thought she was done with babies, there will be all those items she'll need this time around that didn't even exist when she had the "first batch" of kids!

Showers for Unwed Mothers

If your friend is having a baby on her own, she'll probably need even more support and supplies, depending on her economic level. The shower is one chance to really help her out without it looking like charity. A single mother will be lacking any regular help with the baby, most likely, and despite protests in advance, the reality of getting up four times a night and working forty hours a week is that it isn't a whole lot of fun. Wonderful friends like you might pitch in and hire a doula (a woman to come care for mother and baby) for her for the first weeks after the baby is born. Maybe you'll give her a gift certificate to the child care facility she'll be using when she returns to work. You could write little coupons to help her out with things needing to be done around the house, like volunteering to come help her paint the baby's room before its birth. Bring dinner every night for the first six weeks of baby's life. You could all pitch in and hire a maid for her for the first three months of baby's life, or volunteer to drop in and help with laundry and housework yourselves. Give her two cases of disposable diapers. Give her a case of formula if she'll be using it. Give her things that are practical. Anything physically helpful or pleasant is nice, too. Massage appointments, scented candles, facial supplies—anything to help her carve some time for her fatigued self out of the first few months of baby's life on the outside of the womb would be much appreciated!

Showers for Mothers-to-Be Who Are Also About to Marry

Have you ever come to the right place! Between this book and my other, *The Everything Wedding Shower Book,* you can combine the two showers and create something out of this world! What a wonderful opportunity to show your love for the new couple and their new baby! And what a party this will be!

Baby Shower after the New Baby's Sibling Has Died

If this baby is being born after the mother has previously had a miscarriage, a stillborn, or lost another child there's even more reason to have a shower filled with gaiety and love! Assuming it's been a while since the death, she'll probably really appreciate the outpouring of love, support, and encouragement from her friends. Go right ahead—there's no social stigma to it.

What if Something Dreadful Happens?

I read that the infant mortality rate in the early 1800s was such that one out of twenty-six children born would die before adulthood. Thankfully, these statistics are only part of history now, but bad

More Photo Memories

Be sure to take a picture of each guest with the mother-to-be. When developing the film, have double prints made—one for the mother-to-be to keep and one for her to include with the thank you note she will write to each guest for her gift.

And of course, be sure a group photo is taken.

things do happen. In our modern world, babies still die in utero, die at birth, or die shortly after birth. There are miscarriages and infant deaths for a variety of reasons.

I pray along with you that no such tragedy will befall your friend. But if it does, how incredibly important it will be for you to help at this critical time of intense grief. If the mother loses the pregnancy before the shower, I believe it is your responsibility to immediately call your guest list, cancel the shower and tell them why, assuming the grieving family would not be offended by that action. Direct the guests during your phone call to how they may be useful to the family. Cards, flowers, and food sent to the home are typical ways of expressing support and are commonly appreciated.

CHAPTER 3:

Shower Themes

Dream Up a Theme

A themed party would add an interesting twist to your baby shower. There are plenty of traditional showers in the world—the kind where you simply eat cake and watch her open cute baby gifts. There's nothing wrong with that sort of party, but there's also nothing particularly exciting about it, either. You could have done that without this book, so I'm assuming we're looking for something special, yes?

In this section, you'll find all sorts of clever ideas for showers. The ideas are meant to spark your own creativity and give your brain something to chew on. You can always come up with something of your own, or add to the ideas here.

Themed showers are fun for several reasons—the planning is easier; the event is more memorable; the pictures are easy to identify; everyone remembers the event more clearly.

If some of the following stuff sounds too far out, it's no big deal. There are some really conservative ideas tucked in here, too. The idea is that you and your guests and pregnant friend have fun and be comfortable. So browse through these lists and pick and choose what you like. Have your cohost select her three favorite themes. You do the same and choose the one(s) that overlaps.

The theme might well influence where you hold the party and how much you spend, but there are many ways to add a little creativity to the basic pink and blue baby shower.

If you're giving one of several showers for the mother-to-be, you might want to throw a gift-specific party—everyone needs to bring a pink dress or a blue jumpsuit, or furniture for the nursery, traveling-with-baby items, spa items for the expectant mom, or, if the shower is early on in the mother-to-be's pregnancy, even maternity clothes.

If baby's birthday is scheduled on or near a major holiday, have a holiday party a few months early. The new mom probably won't be attending many holiday parties herself, so it will be a nice opportunity for her.

Themes that involve all your guests in something beyond buying a gift and showing up are the best.

For themed surprise parties that include costumes, make sure the mom-to-be's husband either brings something that she already has that suits the theme so she can change, or else make/buy her something to make whatever she's wearing "fit in"—as much as anyone does when wearing a tent!

Ladies High Tea Party

This delightful takeoff on the British tradition of high tea is a charming idea. Serve a true high tea, complete with scones, jam, clotted cream, cucumber sandwiches, and an assortment of teas. Have it outside on a big lawn, and have everyone wear tea gowns (usually, some lightweight, summery ankle-length dress) with big hats.

It's perfect if you can find delightful floral tablecloths, some vases of roses and daisies, lace table toppers, and china cups. (Borrow cups from everyone you know who has china for a festive variety!) As party favors, send your guests home with collections of tea bags, tiny pots of jam, bath tea sachets, floral perfume, or potpourri.

Tea Party Invitations

I have to admit I am stealing this idea for the invitations from a batch of cards I saw in England. Delicately patterned heavyweight paper was cleverly cut into the shape of a teacup and saucer. The paper was outlined in dark blue so you could immediately recognize it as a teacup and saucer shape. A tiny paper strawberry was pasted to the "saucer" part, and an individually wrapped Earl Grey teabag was tucked into a slit cut in the side of the cup. Adorable! The invitations were printed on the inside.

Make the mother-to-be a big sun hat and decorate it with flowers and ribbons you hot-glued on. Remember not to make her cook in the heat—she's more sensitive to heat when she's pregnant than you are now.

Recipe

Baby Shower Scones

You'll need:
3 cups unbleached flour
1 T Baking powder
$\frac{1}{2}$ t. baking soda
$\frac{1}{8}$ t. salt
$\frac{3}{4}$ cup butter
$\frac{1}{2}$ cup milk
$\frac{1}{2}$ cup maple syrup
2 t. vanilla
Cinnamon Cream (recipe follows)
Strawberry jam

Instructions:

1. Preheat oven to 350 degrees.
2. Combine flour, powder, soda, and salt and whisk lightly.
3. Cut in softened butter with a pastry blender or a mixer until it resembles coarse crumbs.
4. In a small bowl, mix together milk, syrup, and vanilla.
5. Add the moist ingredients to the dry and blend thoroughly until a sticky dough is formed. (If it's too hard to stir, add a little more milk.)
6. On a lightly floured surface, knead the dough a few times to increase elasticity.
7. Break into three equal pieces, and pat one piece into a circle about 6 inches across and 1 inch thick.
8. Cut into fourths, making four wedge-shaped pieces. Repeat with other two dough pieces for a total of 12 wedges.
9. Place 1 inch apart on a greased cookie sheet. Bake fifteen to twenty minutes, or until the outside is light golden brown.
10. Serve warm with cream (the recipe follows) and jam.

To make the cream:

You'll need:
1 cup of heavy whipping cream
2 T powdered sugar
$1\frac{1}{2}$ cups of sour cream
2 t. of cinnamon

Instructions:

Whip the cream and the powdered sugar together until soft peaks form.

Add the sour cream and cinnamon, and beat slowly, just until blended.

Store in the fridge until you're ready to use it.

Hawaiian Shower Party

For mothers-to-be who like Hawaii, who hate winter, who are carrying a half-Hawaiian baby, who got pregnant in Hawaii, or for any other reason, this is a perfect idea! Preferably, hold it in the summer, outside. It's a clever, easy to do, interesting party idea. There are more party goods for this kind of shower than probably anything else you could choose. Get lots of flowers and this comes together in a snap!

Muumuus (big, shapeless dresses) on all the female guests will make the mom-to-be feel right at home fashionwise! Flowers in everyone's hair; a lavish, bountiful table with brightly colored candles and flowers; fresh fruit, rice bowls made of scooped-out pineapples, and a roast suckling pig crackling over an open flame in your backyard. Don't forget to put an apple in its mouth before serving it. Oh yeah, and add a dash of "poi"—the yummy (!) Hawaiian "vegetable" made out of some sort of rotting plant. I found a flat plastic lobster that was a wall decoration. For one party, I filled him with red Jell-O and he made a delightful centerpiece. I even found a little mechanical dancing hula girl in a thrift shop and a couple of batteries made her swoon to her own ukulele.

Hand out plastic leis when guests arrive (you can get them very cheap from a place called Oriental Trading Company—see address in the back of this book). Serve fruit punch—spiked and plain, and a main entrée of shish kebabs or sweet-and-sour pineapple meatballs with lots of rice and some Hawaiian bread from the grocery store. Make sure you create the baby carriage watermelon garnish in this book for the party.

Hawaiian Party Invitations

These are so cute you'll want to keep them all yourself! First, gather the following items:

Green tissue paper (like for gifts)
Yellow construction paper
Scissors

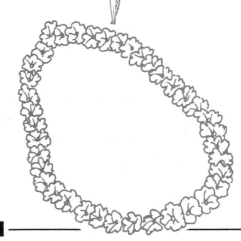

Recipe

Polynesian Meatballs

You'll need:
1 lb. ground beef for each six people
1 c. oatmeal (whole oats)
¼ c. minced onion
salt and pepper to taste
1 egg
¾ c. finely chopped green pepper
½ c. chopped carrots
1 16 oz. can pineapple chunks
1 pint cherry tomatoes (yellow or red)
2 gloves garlic, minced
2 T. cooking oil
½ c. sugar
½ c. red wine vinegar
2 T. soy sauce
2 t. instant chicken bouillon granules
4 T. cornstarch
Hot cooked rice

Instructions:

1. Make meatballs by combining meat, egg, oats, salt and pepper, and minced onion in a large bowl. Mix together thoroughly. Form into 1 inch balls.
2. Brown meatballs on all sides thoroughly, until no pink shows in the center.
3. Combine pepper, carrots, and garlic and cook in oil until tender.
4. Add sugar, vinegar, soy, bouillon, pineapple (including juice), and 2 c. water. Add tomatoes.
5. Bring to rapid boil for one minute.
6. Mix cornstarch in ¼ cup of cold water and stir into hot mixture until thick and bubbly.
7. Just before serving, add cooked meatballs to sauce and stir thoroughly.
8. Serve over fresh steamed rice. Wonderful!

Hot glue gun
Brown marker
Large square envelopes (all the same size)—one for each
    invitation
Paper umbrella toothpicks—one for each invitation

Step 1: From the yellow construction paper, measure a pineapple shape (sort of a lumpy oval) about 2 inches smaller lengthwise than the envelope. (This is so the pineapple fits inside with its top on.)

Step 2: Fold the yellow paper in half with the crease along the top of the pineapple. Cut out the pineapple, leaving the crease intact so the pineapple shape folds open.

Step 3: Decorate the front of the construction paper with brown criss-crosses to resemble the skin of a pineapple. (If you want to get super fancy, do it with brown watercolor paint—mix all the colors together to make brown. But don't use much water as construction paper absorbs too fast!)

Step 4: Make the pineapple leaves by taking the folded tissue paper, drawing a top on it slightly bigger than the pineapple shape and not more than 2 inches tall, and cutting them all out at the same time. (Kind of like the way we made paper dolls when we were little, but make sure you cut all the edges so they separate completely!)

Step 5: Affix two or three to the top page of each pineapple with hot glue. Be careful! It's hot and the paper instantly absorbs the heat!

Step 6: Use a computer and printer to make, or handwrite or type and photocopy, little inserts with the details on them on yellow paper to cut out and glue into the inside of the invitation.

Step 7: Tape, hot glue, or skewer a folded umbrella to the front of each invitation.

Ta-daa! You did it!

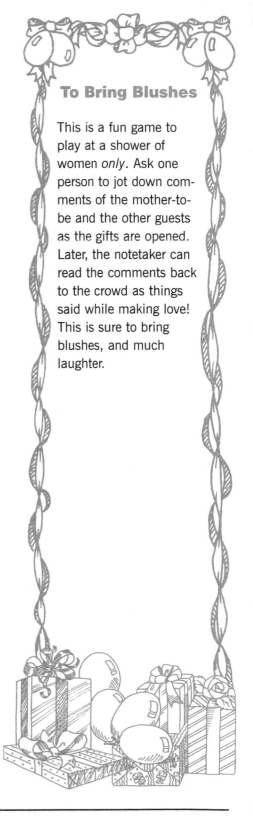

To Bring Blushes

This is a fun game to play at a shower of women *only*. Ask one person to jot down comments of the mother-to-be and the other guests as the gifts are opened. Later, the notetaker can read the comments back to the crowd as things said while making love! This is sure to bring blushes, and much laughter.

Costume Party

Why not invite the guys, too, and turn this into a real festive event? Make everyone come as a famous couple from history—Romeo and Juliet, Henry VIII and Anne Boleyn (with her head still on), Anthony and Cleopatra, Frankenstein and his bride, and so on. Make sure you either rent a costume for the mother-to-be or tell her in advance! Or you could make everyone show up "pregnant," with giant balloons under their dresses!

Costume parties are fun because they somehow free a lot of people psychologically. Dressed as someone else, some folks let down their guard and just relax into the role.

If you want to turn it into a masquerade party, everyone would wear masks until midnight, when they would remove them all at once and discover at last who is who! You might choose to provide the masks for this, as party favors.

Exciting invitations would be to cut mask shapes (like the Lone Ranger's) from heavy-stock colored paper. Use glitter glue and feathers to decorate each mask and write the details on the back. Punch holes in the sides, apply "hole reinforcers" from the stationery store (those little Tyvek rings that strengthen hole punches so they don't rip), and pull through some ribbon on either side so they tie in the back. You'll be the hostest with the mostest, especially if you come as Elvira!

Recipe

Costume Party Cookies

You'll need:
2 c. white flour
1½ t. baking powder
6 T butter at room temperature
⅓ c. shortening
¾ c. sugar
1 egg
1 T. milk
1½ t. vanilla
Red and blue food coloring
Candy ornaments—red hots, M&M's, metallic balls, etc.
A paring knife

Instructions:
1. In a big bowl, stir together flour, baking powder, and a pinch of salt.
2. In another bowl, mix together butter and shortening. Add sugar and beat until well mixed.
3. To the moist ingredients, add egg, milk, and vanilla. Beat well.
4. Add the moist to the dry ingredients and mix well.
5. Cover with a plate and chill about two hours.
6. Preheat oven to 375 degrees.
7. Roll dough to half-inch thickness. Using the paring knife, cut small mask shapes from the dough, using a pair of sunglasses as a guide if it seems hard to do freehand.
8. Decorate with gewgaws. Put colorful candy items around the frames of the masks.
9. Bake six to eight minutes or until done. Makes about eighteen to twenty-four cookies.

Costuming Your Pregnant Friend

What better thing can she come as than . . . The Great Pumpkin?!? What a GREAT idea! This costume is VERY easy, even if you don't sew. (You can do it with staples and hot glue if you want!)

Go to the fabric store and buy

- 4 yards of bright orange fabric, at least 54 inches wide.
- 3 squares of green felt
- A hot glue gun if you cannot sew
- A piece of yarn (green or orange)

Step1: Cut the fabric into four yard-long pieces. (A yard is three feet)

Step 2: Sew or hot glue three pieces together to form a solid panel.

Step 3: Sew or hot glue the third piece halfway up, skip 8 inches, sew or hot glue the rest (this is to get her hands out). You now have a giant orange tube, open at the bottom and top.

Step 4: Cut two pieces of green felt into three long triangles each. Iron 2 inches of the top of the orange fabric tube over, as if it were a hem. Either sew, pin, or hot glue it along the very edge so it stays in place. You are creating the neckline for the pumpkin. Take the piece of yarn and thread it through the hem you've created to make a drawstring.

Step 5: With the drawstring partly closed (put it over your head to test it!) hot glue the pumpkin leaves of green felt around the neck.

Step 6: Do the drawstring thing along the bottom of the "tube" also. Don't worry, she and baby will make the pumpkin shape fill out just fine.

Step 7: If you want, you can draw ridges along the outside of the pumpkin with a brown marker.

Step 8: With the remaining piece of green felt, make a nifty cap by cutting a 6-inch high, 4-inch long strip off the edge. Roll the strip into a sturdy stem and hot glue it so it doesn't unroll. Cut a ragged edge around the remainder of the felt, and hot glue the stem to the middle. With bobby pins, her chic cap will stay in place.

Western Hoedown

Why not have everyone wear Western wear or even square-dancing costumes? Could you invite guys, too, and hire a square-dance caller and someone to teach y'all how to dosey-do in your spacious backyard? How about line dancing? Or do you just want to play Garth Brooks on the CD player and have the guests wear their boots? You'd probably serve a red-meat barbecue—no tofu for this crowd! Or maybe chili, and you could send everyone home with a little package of chili mix as a party favor. (Make sure you have non-spicy entrees, too, for the mother-to-be and particular guests!)

You could provide everyone with a neckerchief in bright colors—many hobby stores carry them for as little as ninety-nine cents each. You could use a few bales of hay for seating in your backyard.

For clever invitations, buy some brown construction paper, some small chicken feathers (or pull them from a pillow), and a small square of fake leather, leopard skin, or calico fabric. Cut the construction paper into little cowboy hat shapes, leaving the top of the hat with a seam so that it flips opens like a card. Cut the fabric into tiny strips to make hatbands and glue the feathers into the hatband. On the inside, insert the actual wording of the invitation. Yee-haw!

Hint: Check out The Everything Barbecue Book *for some lip-smackin' recipes sure to warm the cockles o' your hearts!*

Recipe

World's Best Corn Bread

I've made this recipe so many times, I could do it in my sleep! It's going to be a hit at the party, and you'll probably come back here again and again to make it for no special occasion.

You'll need:
½ c. whole wheat flour
½ c. white flour
1 c. yellow cornmeal (I use coarsely ground)
¼ c. white sugar
4 t. baking powder
2 eggs
1 c. milk
¼ c. corn oil
½ c. corn kernels
Pimentos (optional)
honey

Instructions:

1. Preheat oven to 425 degrees.

2. Stir together flours, cornmeal, sugar, baking powder, and a pinch of salt.

3. Add eggs, milk, oil, corn, and pimentos.

4. Stir until smooth, and pour into a greased 9 x 9 x 2 pan.

5. Bake for twenty to twenty-five minutes.

6. When slightly cooled, drizzle with honey and serve with butter.

Pirates of Penzance

How about a Pirate Shower? What a great idea! You can sail the seven seas right from your own living room! Here's how to make your swashbuckling friends never forget this one!

I'd buy some red kerchiefs (one per person), some cheapo junky gold clip-on ring earrings from the deep discount store, a black eyebrow pencil, and a collection of little boys' plastic swords. If you invite the guys to this one, it might be even more charming. Tell everyone to dress as a pirate, with white shirts and with full skirts tied with scarves for the women. You provide each guest with a kerchief, an earring, and a chance to apply a swarthy complexion with your eyebrow pencil. Give them a sword for a real swashbuckling time. What fun!

You could wrap each invitation around a sword and mail or deliver it—which'd be cute! Or you could mail the invitation on yellowed paper wrapped in a kerchief. Here's a recipe to yellow regular paper. Watch it SO carefully to be sure it doesn't burn!

Take a sheet of white or pale yellow cotton laid paper (not cheap copy paper!) and print your invitation on it. Add a map and mark where your house is with a big red X. Cut or tear the edges to make it look old. Smear each invitation with butter (no kidding!) and lay it flat on a cookie sheet. Place in oven for a few minutes at 200 degrees—WATCH them so they don't burn!

Voila! You have "aged" your paper and are ready to send a real treasure map!

For The Gift Table

Ooh! This is so much fun! Go behind an appliance store and steal for yourself an empty dishwasher box. You're a pirate, after all! (If you stole one with the dishwasher still in it, you'd be a real pirate and I'd get sued, which would anger my publisher rather badly.)

Make the box into a square again (if it's been flattened) and seal it. Now, grab a can of flat brown spray paint. Paint the whole box so you cannot read the label anymore. When it's dry, take a box knife or an Exacto knife, and cut the box open on three sides to form a "lid" that's attached on one side. The lip of the lid

Recipe

Peppermint Patties

You'll need:
2 lbs. of powdered sugar
6 T. light corn syrup
6 T. water
1 t. peppermint extract
Red food coloring
Blue food coloring

Instructions:

1. Combine the sugar, corn syrup, and water in the top of a double boiler. (If you don't have a double boiler, use a thin skillet on top of a Dutch oven. The idea of a double boiler is that the steam from the pot below heats the pot above indirectly. The upper pot, containing the ingredients, never touches the heat.)
2. Simmer the water below, but don't let it boil. Stir upper concoction until sugar dissolves and mixture is smooth.
3. Remove from heat, but leave the skillet over the water so it stays warm.
4. Stir in the peppermint extract.
5. Halve mixture. To one half add red coloring and stir until it becomes pink. For the other half, add blue.
6. Drop onto cookie sheets to form 1 inch pools. Chill until firm. If you want, you could press a plastic baby or a rattle into a few of them to decorate them. Make sure whatever you add is so obvious no one eats it!
7. Just before placing the treasure box on the table for your centerpiece, add the mints. Lovely!

should be at least 3 inches, in other words, cut down three inches from the box top all around on three sides.

Spray some masking tape or duct tape bright gold. Apply that to the seam of the lid, and also use it to decorate the box. You can cut a broken lock out of black construction paper, and you can make the box more "woodlike" by drawing nails and wood grain on the outside with a black marker.

Your guests will place all the booty assembled "fer tha fair lass and wee bairn" to this lavish repository. In other words, put the gifts inside.

Treasure Chest

For this edible table decoration, you'll need:

A collection of either gold foil–covered chocolate coins or homemade pink and blue peppermints (the recipe follows)

6 Ring Pops—ask any elementary school kid if you don't know what they are

6 candy necklaces

A shoe box with a lid

Gold paint

Flat Brown spray paint

A black marker (see "for the Gift Table" instructions above for these three items)

A piece of red velvet big enough to cover the entire interior of the box and its lid

A few stick-on jewels from the crafts store

Instructions:

1. Masking tape one side of the lid to the box to form a lid that opens but doesn't detach.
2. When you are spray-painting the treasure gift chest above, spray paint the outside of the shoebox, too, including the lid.
3. When the box is dry, cut and glue red velvet to the inside to form the lining.
4. Using gold paint, glue, and the fake gemstones, decorate the outside of the treasure chest. Use the black marker to draw

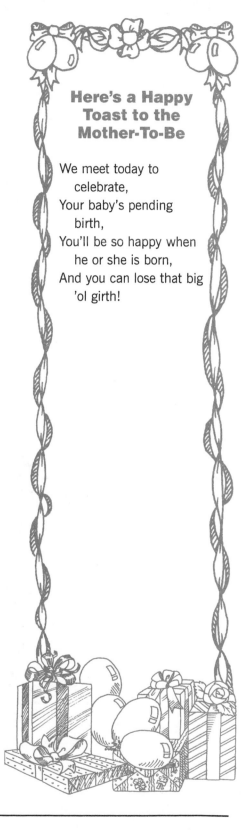

Here's a Happy Toast to the Mother-To-Be

We meet today to
    celebrate,
Your baby's pending
    birth,
You'll be so happy when
    he or she is born,
And you can lose that big
    'ol girth!

wood grain and nails on the box; use the gold paint to form hinges. Allow to dry.

5. Fill the box with goodies—the candy necklaces and Ring Pops unwrapped, and also the chocolate coins. To make your own coins in blue and pink, follow the clever recipe below for peppermint patties.

Stork Shower

Did you know that, long ago, storks delivered babies? At least, that's what little Scandinavian kids were told when the storks roosted above their chimneys. How thoughtful of the storks to save those women nine months of pregnancy and all the hassles of labor! As homage to those kindly birds, why not have a stork shower?

You'll find six zillion stork objects at the party goods store. Think of the Vlasic pickle bird, and you'll see a stork. They are in truth very pretty birds, although their mythological role in child bearing seems a little far-fetched. I don't know about you, but if we can go back to the stork method, I'd prefer it.

For this party, you'd of course get all the stork stuff you can find, but also look for small white artificial birds. Chances are, you can find them at a crafts store. It'd be pretty cute to scroll up the invitation and wire it to the bird's feet. Delivered by a stork! You could write a code or a word on the bottom of one, and give a prize to the guest who comes with her stork. You could give a prize to the guest who shows up with the most creative use or portrayal of her stork (perched on the edge of her eyeglasses, in a creative hair-do, etc.).

For cute party favors, why not take little pink and blue tulle circles with candy or nuts in them, and tie them to the storks' beaks? You could tie matching ribbons around their necks.

Recipe

Babycakes Stork Shower Cake

You'll need:

1 pound cake (recipe follows)
1 plastic doll head, about 4 inches in diameter (you can find disembodied dolls anywhere from Kmart to the crafts store)
One set of doll legs and one set of arms
A clean white handkerchief
A diaper pin
A length of pink or blue fabric, cut 18 inches long x 8 inches wide
One paper stork (see resources section at the end of this book)
Some fishing line (fine gauge) or white silk thread
A tube of decorating gel
1 pt. whipping cream
½ c. white sugar
Fresh berries, in season

Instructions:

1. Bake and cool cake according to directions below.
2. When the cake is cool, poke the head into the small end of the pound cake and the arms into the sides so they point more up than out. Poke in the legs so they point up and out. In other words, the baby should be lying on its back, arms up and legs out.
3. Fold a small piece of aluminum foil the size of the bottom of the cake and place under the baby.
4. "Diaper" the baby, too, with a clean white handkerchief. Use a real diaper pin to seal.
5. Write with decorating gel "Welcome Baby!" across the baby's stomach.
6. Place the length of fabric under the baby to form a sling, which you will now tie to the paper stork's beak with the thread or fishing line. Obviously, the paper stork only appears to be supporting the weight of the cake baby.

Recipe

6-Pound Bouncing Baby Cake

You'll need:
½ lb. butter (room temperature)
1⅔ c. sugar
5 eggs
2 c. white flour
1 t. vanilla
Zest of one lemon

Instructions:

1. Preheat oven to 325 degrees. Butter and lightly flour a loaf pan (9" x 5")
2. Cream the butter with the sugar, slowly adding the sugar.
3. Add the eggs one at a time, beating well after each addition.
4. Stir in the flour, pinch of salt, vanilla, and lemon zest and combine well.
5. Scrape into pan and bake for about 1½ hours or until it tests done.
6. Cool five minutes before removing from pan. Cool completely on wire rack.

To Serve the Babycakes:

Take scissors decorated with pink and blue ribbon and cut open the sling, to reveal the entire baby inside (only the head and feet have been poking out until now!).

Slice the cake and generously load with berries and cream. A delightful, unexpected, and refreshing idea for a shower cake-without the heavy frosting!

Bun in the Oven Party

Here's a fun idea! Not too long ago, Americans used to euphemistically call being pregnant "having a bun in the oven." For this shower, serve fresh warm buns. Invite all the guests to bring either a homemade complete frozen meal for the new family to thaw and eat in those hectic first weeks, or a coupon promising to deliver a meal to their home when the baby comes. What could be more appreciated? Probably nothing! Buy her one of those cheap Styrofoam coolers to take it all home in. She'll love you for this!

Bun in the Oven Party Centerpiece

You'll need:

An 8" square box
White spray paint
An Exacto or box knife
A piece of cellophane wrap
Aluminum foil
Glue
Red yarn
Black construction paper or a small strip of clear black plastic
4 tiny silver or white buttons (¼ inch wide maximum)
4 straight pins
Hot glue
A small piece of aluminum foil

Step 1. Spray paint the box and allow it to dry thoroughly.

Step 2: Leaving a one inch margin, cut an "oven door" into one side using the knife. Cut it only on three sides. Pull to open the oven door. Cut a smaller "window" into the door. Tape the cellophane wrap over the inside of the window.

Step 3: Cut four 3-inch long pieces of red yarn. With clear glue, like Elmer's, draw a swirl (think electric burner) in four places on the oven top. Apply the red yarn and allow to dry.

Step 4: Make the back plate of the stove by slicing and then stapling in place the leftover cutout cardboard from the oven

window. Along this back, tape or glue the black plastic or construction paper. (You could use exposed film to make the back of the oven.)

Step 5: Either along the front or on the black back plate, attach the button "knobs" by pushing the pin through one of the holes, thus affixing the knob in place. Or, you could just hot glue them on, but they won't turn.

Step 6: Mold aluminum foil to make an oven door handle. Hot glue in place.

Step 7: Make sure to place one of your fresh buns inside the oven, on an overturned box, to complete the effect!

Make hot cross buns, cross them with pink and blue frosting, and stick a diaper pin in the middle of them. To do that, you'll need:

At least one bun recipe (follows)

Pink and blue frosting (follows)

A corresponding number of pins (the following recipe makes eighteen buns)

You could order everyone to wear their hair in a bun. You could play a game where you bring pictures of baby buns and try to guess whose are whose from the "bear rug" pictures, OR you could (if you're the more daring type) bring in every picture you can find of male celebrity buns and THEN have a bun-identification contest. Which brings up the subject of moon pies. Or not.

Recipe

Bun in the Oven Buns

3½ c. white flour
2 packages of active dry yeast
½ t. cinnamon
¼ t. ground cloves
¾ c. milk
½ c. oil
⅓ c. sugar
3 eggs
⅔ c. golden raisins, currants, or chopped diced dried cherries
1 egg white, slightly beaten
1½ c. powdered sugar (sift to remove any lumps)
¼ t. vanilla
Red and blue food coloring

Instructions:

1. In a large mixing bowl, combine 1½ c. flour, yeast, cinnamon, and cloves. Stir well. Turn on oven to 350 degrees for two minutes exactly. Turn off oven.
2. In a saucepan, heat milk, oil, sugar, and a few pinches of salt until warm. Stir constantly.
3. Add milk mixture to flour mixture. Add eggs and beat at low speed about 30 seconds until completely combined.
4. Beat 2½ minutes at high speed. Stir in dried fruit and as much of the remaining flour as you can stir in with a spoon.
5. Toss dough onto lightly floured surface and knead in more flour to make a smooth, elastic dough. (This may take as long as six minutes. Just think! It's cheaper than going to the gym!)
6. Shape dough into a ball, place back in mixing bowl, and cover with a towel. Place in warm—but not on—oven and allow to rise until double (about 1½ hours).
7. At this point, you're probably thinking, "Thank heavens for bread machines. I've got to get one!"
8. Remove from oven. Punch down dough. Turn onto the same lightly floured surface and cover. Let it nap for ten minutes.
9. Divide dough into eighteen pieces. Roll each piece into a smooth ball. Place on greased cookie sheet about 2 inches apart.
10. Cover. Let them rise until double their original size. This will take about thirty or forty-five minutes. Halfway through their rest, preheat the oven to 375 degrees.
11. With a sharp knife, slash a shallow cross on the top of each. (You'll later fill this with frosting.) Brush tops with a pastry brush dipped in some of the slightly beaten egg white.
12. Bake at 375 degrees for twelve to fifteen minutes, or until golden.
13. In a bowl, mix powdered sugar, vanilla, and the rest of the egg white. Halve the frosting. To one half, add red food coloring to get pink, to the other, blue.
14. If the frosting is too stiff, add a little milk. Make designs on the tops of the cooled buns.

Teddy Bear Party

If the mom-to-be likes bears, or thinks they'd be cute in her baby's nursery, have all the guests bring a teddy bear (or a stuffed penguin, iguana, monkey, whatever animal she's most into) to the party in addition to their gift. She could end up with a whole wonderful collection for the baby!

You could decorate the room, the cake and the invitations with cute little teddy bears. Get a teddy bear metal cookie cutter from the specialty food store and use it to cut cute canapés in bear shapes. (Make cold cut sandwiches by layering three pieces of inexpensive store-bought wheat or white bread spread with something like mayo, and cut them to shape. Don't try to use a plastic cookie cutter—they stick badly to white bread. Use cheap bread because it cuts easier. The better grades won't.)

You just have to make the Teddy Bear cake.

Nursery Décor Party

If she's chosen a theme for the nursery—little yellow duckies, Winnie the Pooh, pink and green ribbons, Teletubbies, Barney or anything else, you could decorate your house/party accordingly and have guests bring things that carry that theme. Just tell them on the invitations that that's what she's doing, and where to get the stuff. Most likely a major chain store like JC Penney (which has a good line of brand baby linens) or some similar place will have exactly what you and your guests need.

To decorate the party accordingly, you might want to use crib sheets as table coverings, receiving blankets as basket liners for dry goods (like bread rolls), and the character or animal as a centerpiece on both the gift and the food tables. The animal could be holding a collection of matching balloons. If you open or use these items before giving them to her, make sure you wash them before you actually make a gift of them. Most major lines will also have matching party goods and invitations, et cetera, to help promote themselves. If you've never looked around, you'll be amazed what you can find.

Recipe

Teddy Bear Cake

You'll need:

Two packages chocolate cake mix, prepared
Two containers of chocolate frosting
1 long piece of wide candy ribbon (fruit rolls, sour tape taffy, tape bubble gum, etc.)
3 pieces of pink bubble gum (not the kind with syrup inside!)
3 paper liners for muffin pan
2 Oreo-style cookies
2 chocolate drops

Step 1: Bake cake according to directions in a large round cake pan. Also bake three cupcakes. Freeze when cool.

Step 2: Take cakes out to thaw about five hours before the party. Take long strips of aluminum foil and edge your cake platter or plate with them, about 1 inch under the cake itself. Place the cake on the platter, with two cupcake "ears" above.

Step 3: Frost the whole thing with the chocolate frosting.

Step 4: Turn the third cupcake upside down slightly below the center of the bear's face to form his nose.

Step 5: Frost the nose. (The reason you didn't put the nose on in the beginning is because the frosting under it helps it stick on.)

Step 6: Unwrap the bubble gum and put it in a teensy amount of water in a saucer in the microwave for a few seconds to make it soft. Press it into a nose shape and inner ears for the teddy bear. Apply to cake.

Step 7: Form a bow with the tape candy for the teddy's neck. Open both Oreo cookies and place these eyes white side up on the bear. Use the chocolate drops to form the irises. (Eat the part without the frosting. I know that's not the yummy part, but you cannot buy just two Oreos, so you can finish the rest of the bag while you're finishing the cake.)

Step 8: Make him a little pink or red tongue out of the remaining candy tape. You can make him whiskers with black licorice if you like, but he's probably pretty cute already. Chill and remove the aluminum foil when the frosting is set so that the cake plate is clean.

Recipe

Teddy Bear Sandwiches

Here's where you get to try your hand at even more creativity. If you want to make the bread dough by hand, or in your bread machine (but not bake it in the machine), I recommend you look at your cookbook. I'm going to assume you already have a lump of room temperature or warmer bread dough in your hot little hands when I give you these directions, OK?

You'll need:
A loaf-sized piece of uncooked, warm bread dough (from your grocer's freezer, your own Suzy Homemaker skill set, or fresh from the bread machine on "dough" setting (my preferred method!)
The whites of two eggs, slightly beaten
6 whole cloves
A length of red ribbon
Ripe tomatoes
Freshly washed lettuce
Cold cuts (a variety)
Mayo, mustard (a couple of different kinds), pickles
Any other sandwich stuff you think is good to eat

Here's what you do with the bread dough:

With about half the dough, form a long oval body for the teddy bear.
With about half the remaining dough, give him a head.
Use the remaining dough to add legs, arms, ears, and a nice nose.
Brush the entire bear with the egg whites. (He may giggle like the Pillsbury dough boy, but don't worry about that!)
Poke three cloves into each side of his face to form his eyes.
Bake according to package or recipe instructions.
He'll come out golden brown.
When he's cool, tie the red ribbon around his neck.
Serve with a large bread knife, so he can be eaten horizontally or vertically.
Surround him with sandwich fixings.

Isn't that cute?

Ten minutes ago in the greeting card section of my local drugstore, I found a whole collection of cheap resin Winnie the Pooh pins—they weren't near any other Winnie the Pooh items that I could find, but there they were. America is a mecca for merchandising ancillary products.

Nursery Lamp Project

If your friend is having a girl, and you know what color she is painting the nursery, you're in luck. Buy a lamp or get a used one and paint the base. I'll assume you're doing it in pink. If you're not, alter accordingly. A boy's lamp and a neutral lamp idea follow.

Rose Lamp

You'll need:

A used or new small lamp with a wooden base

Pink spray paint

A hot glue gun with glue

Pink ribbon or fringe (fabric stores stock this stuff)—enough to trim the circumference of the bottom of the lamp shade

At least two dozen pink *polyester* roses, peonies, or other flowers

At least one dozen small white *polyester* flowers (daisies, stephanotis, etc.)

Step 1: Masking tape or wrap aluminum foil over the cord of the lamp from the base down about 1 foot. Cover the mechanism, too, and any exposed metal parts. This is so these don't get paint on them in Step 2.

Step 2: Spray paint the base baby pink. Allow to dry.

Step 3: Pop the blooms off of all your flowers and pile them in a big bowl. Plug in the glue gun.

Step 4: Glue your trim, braid, cording, or ribbon to the bottom edge of the lamp shade.

Step 5: Randomly glue the blooms all over the shade until the entire shade is covered. DO NOT glue any blooms so high up on the shade that their petals can catch on fire or melt by sinking into the lamp itself when it's been on a long time!

Step 6: Reassemble the lamp, insert a pink mood lightbulb, and voila! You're done!

Little Boy's Lamp

If you know what theme she's chosen for his nursery, you're in great luck! Is it cowboys? Ducks? Geometric patterns? American flags? Here's what to do:

Step 1: Trip on down to the fabric store and find fabric that matches her theme in the novelty prints section. Buy some matching trim and some Ailene's Tacky Glue.

Step 2: Using a lamp with a wood base, spray paint the wood as described in Steps 1 and 2 for the Rose Lamp. A lamp with a burlap shade might be cute for cowboys. You can buy shades separately at the hardware store.

Step 3: Carefully cut out the desired images from the fabric with sharp scissors.

Step 4: If the images won't cover the entire shade and you don't want to leave it white, you can spray paint it lightly. Otherwise, use the glue to affix the fabric images to the lampshade. Then hot glue the trim to the bottom of the shade.

Step 5: Reassemble the lamp—voila! How cute!

Geometric Lamp for Baby's Room
You'll need:

A metal-based lamp in white or a primary color

A solid heavyweight paper shade or a sturdy fabric one

Lengths of primary-colored ribbons with various textures—grosgrain, satin, satin with looped edges, etc.

A hot glue gun with glue

Step 1: Take the shade off the lamp and plan out your design. Glue strips of ribbon vertically and horizontally around the shade, weaving them over and under one another for effect.

Step 2: While the shade dries, take three of the primary colors and hot glue them up the stalk of the lamp base. Wrap other ribbons around them if desired to cover the entire stalk.

Step 3: Reassemble. You're done!

If you're handy, you might even want to try this. Where I live, there's a craze for decorated lampshades. It's not as hard as you think, and a decorated nursery lamp would be a wonderful gift for you to give her. Make it the centerpiece of the table decorations.

The Gala Event Party

You know, it might be a while before she gets out with her husband again. Especially for a night on the town without worrying about the babysitter and her precious darling home alone together.

If you can spring for it, why not do a final gala event for your friend? Complete with a caterer and rented location, this is an elegant, tasteful, classy party for your chic mother-to-be. Hosted at a local hotel, this party includes men, champagne, a sit-down dinner, and a super cake. Lots of fun, rather pricey, but worth it. Have your guests dress formally or semiformally. See if you can get a band or a harpist to provide live music for the event.

See the sections later on hiring a caterer and leasing a location. The fees and costs even within your city limits will vary greatly. See what you can do nicely and inexpensively.

For a really clever and elegant invitation, try buying some glossy black paper from the art supply store. With a thin line of glue, write the mother-to-be's name or the words "Black Tie Baby Shower" on paper you've cut and folded in half. Sprinkle the wet glue with gold glitter. Or get a fancy stamp and a gold glitter stamp pad and stamp the fronts. On the inside, insert a piece of tissue paper in the colors of the shower, or ask the mother-to-be if she has leftovers from the invitations. Print the words of the invitation on the inside.

Send each female attendee home with a long-stemmed rose from the table bouquets, or a fancy sachet filled with Jordan almonds in a veil bag tied with gold curling ribbon. It's not your typical baby shower, but who says you have to be typical?

You're going to need centerpieces for the tables for this event. See if your location will allow you to bring your own. If they do, may I suggest the following?

What you will need:
Cheap baby bottles (as many as there will be tables at your event)
Gold florist's foil (available not only at flower shops, where it will be marked up, but also at some crafts stores and all florist supply stores)
Black, gold, and silver metallic curling ribbon

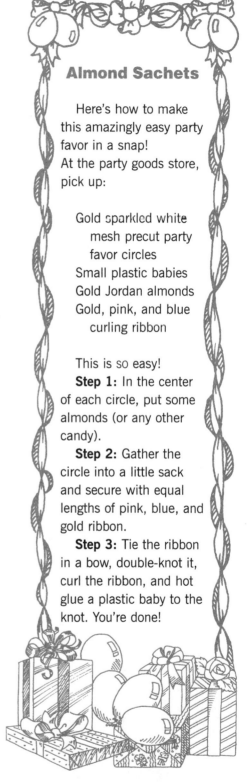

Almond Sachets

Here's how to make this amazingly easy party favor in a snap! At the party goods store, pick up:

Gold sparkled white mesh precut party favor circles
Small plastic babies
Gold Jordan almonds
Gold, pink, and blue curling ribbon

This is so easy!
Step 1: In the center of each circle, put some almonds (or any other candy).
Step 2: Gather the circle into a little sack and secure with equal lengths of pink, blue, and gold ribbon.
Step 3: Tie the ribbon in a bow, double-knot it, curl the ribbon, and hot glue a plastic baby to the knot. You're done!

Instructions:

1. Take a baby bottle, assembled with the nipple on, and wrap it tightly in gold foil. Smooth it out using a blunt wooden object, like a wooden spoon or a pencil.
2. Wrap long strands (two or three of each color) of curling ribbon around the neck of each bottle. Curl the ribbon by stretching the ribbon between your thumb and a knife or scissor blade quickly.
3. Hot glue regular straws to the base of each bottle.
4. Poke a long bamboo skewer through each straw quickly, before the hot glue cools, with the pointy end out the bottom.
5. Insert a bottle into each flower arrangement on each table.

Southwest Fiesta Shower

There's a niño on the way! Let's party, amigo! Not much is easier to cook for a crowd than Mexican food. Whether it's appetizers or a main course, Mexican food is easy to cook, easy to serve, and always popular. Throw some corn chips in a bowl with two or three kinds of salsa (or look under "Quick Catering" for a great bean dip recipe!). Play Mexican music, decorate with sombreros and serapes (Mexican colorful woven blankets), and hire some mariachis to come play for your group. You can send the guests home with little loaves of cornbread wrapped in "Mexican"-print fabrics. Don't forget to play some great Mexican music!

Fiesta Niño Invitations

For charming invitations, you could make paper flowers out of crepe paper and attach the invitation to the stem. Here's how to do it. You'll want to use 5" x 7" envelopes to mail these.

1. Cut six pear-shaped, pear-sized petals for each invitation out of brightly colored crepe paper (from the hobby/craft store). Don't use tissue paper.

Recipe

Food is so easy for a Mexican feast! Here's my favorite recipe for a super-sized platter of wonderful enchiladas. Serve with corn that's been mixed with a few bits of chopped red pepper (for color), some Spanish rice, and some sour cream and guacamole.

Super Grande Enchildas

You'll need:
2 dozen corn tortillas
½ lb. cheddar cheese, grated
1 onion, chopped
2 green peppers, julienne sliced
1 lb. shredded cooked chicken or ground beef (optional)
10 oz. Ricotta cheese
3 c. enchilada sauce (recipe follows)

Instructions:
1. Brown meat or chicken with onions and green pepper in a large skillet.
2. Stir in ricotta and cheddar cheeses.
3. Prepare sauce and pour just enough to cover the bottom of a 9" x 9" x 2" baking dish. (You'll need two of these dishes, or one very large aluminum foil disposable pan to make this recipe.)
4. In a shallow frying pan, heat oil 'til sizzling.
5. Dip each tortilla in oil for a few seconds, until limp.
6. Place tortilla flat into the sauce, coating both sides.
7. When six tortillas have been lightly fried in this manner, assemble each by spooning a few tablespoons of filling into each.
8. Roll so that the seam faces down and stays in place.
9. When the entire base of the baking dish has been lined with stuffed, rolled enchiladas, pour sauce over the row and sprinkle with a little cheese, if desired.
10. For remaining enchiladas, use next baking dish, or you can layer the rows, but they will not look as pretty when you serve them as if you did it only one deep.

To prepare sauce:
You'll need:
2 T. chopped onion
4 cloves garlic, minced
4 T. chili powder
2 14-oz. cans of chicken broth, with the fat removed
3 c. canned chopped tomatoes
2 T. cornstarch
4 t. apple cider vinegar
A pinch or two of salt

Instructions:
1. Sauté garlic and onion a few seconds in a little oil in a skillet.
2. Add ½ c. of the broth and all of the chili powder and simmer for a minute or two.
3. Pour the mixture into a blender and blend until it's smooth. Add the chopped tomatoes and blend until smooth.
4. Pour the blended sauce back into the saucepan and add the remaining broth.
5. Mix the cornstarch into 4 T of water and the vinegar. Stir into the sauce until it is thickened slightly.
6. Add salt to taste.
7. Cool before using. Store any excess for future use—can be frozen.

2. Roll the petals one by one around a pencil width-wise, from end to end, NOT from the tip of the pear shape to the widest part.

3. Unroll the petals and gather them together at the narrowest part of the shape with a green pipe cleaner in the center. Scrunch them together and wrap some of the pipe cleaner around the petals. This now forms the stamen of the flower and the back of the green pipe cleaner is the stem. Dip this protruding tip into a touch of red paint you've mixed with glue and sprinkle it with green or yellow glitter, or cracked pepper. When dry, attach an invitation printed on heavy-weight paper with a hole punched in the corner to the end of the pipe cleaner.

Totally Cool California Shower, Dude!

Is the baby going to be born in California? Are the parents moving there? Coming from there? Why not have a party based on the stereotypes of the West Coast? Offer your guests plastic sunglasses when they arrive, and have them dress Rodeo Drive gaudy or totally beach bum. The food? Heck, that's easy! Serve braised tofu with rice, and a main dish they'll recognize, too. Lots of sprouts, vegetables, whole grain breads, and so on. The drinks must include fruit punch, sparkling water, and smoothies!

Have the party at a local water park or by your pool. Of course, you'll play Beach Boys music! Heck, why not hire a couple of local beach bum–looking kids to help you serve food and drinks at the party?

Make invitations by sticking contact paper to manila envelopes. Cut them out in the shape of surfboards (like, wow, man!) and paste a printed sheet of data on the "belly" of the board. Totally awesome! You could send your guests home with tiny seashells pressed into white, pink, or blue votive candles you slightly melted. How about little bottles of sunscreen? Beach balls? Totally cool, dude!

Recipe

Braised Tofu with Rice

Ingredients:
1 lb. tofu for each three adults
8 oz. Tamari or low-sodium soy sauce per 2 lbs. of tofu
Green onions
½ teaspoon ginger
½ teaspoon garlic
½ c. uncooked short grain brown rice per person

Step 1: Slice tofu into ¼-inch slabs. Lay flat in shallow baking dish.

Step 2: Mix 2 gloves crushed fresh garlic and ¼ t. ground ginger with 4 oz. Tamari sauce. Pour over tofu slabs. Turn each slab once every four hours. Allow to marinate at least eight hours.

Step 3: Finely chop green onion and sprinkle atop tofu slabs. Bake at 350 degrees for thirty minutes, watching that all the Tamari absorbs but that the tofu doesn't get too dry.

Step 4: Serve warm with extra Tamari sauce and fresh cooked rice. Yummy!

Recipe

Totally California Green Salad

For the salad you'll need:
Salad greens, including alfalfa sprouts
½ c. sunflower seeds, roasted, salted, and shelled
Sliced or wedged tomatoes

For the dressing you'll need:
Mix ½ c. extra virgin olive oil with ½ c. balsamic vinegar
Add ⅛ t. of each of the following:
Dried basil
Garlic powder
Onion salt
Fresh black pepper
Crushed mint

Mix and stir thoroughly. Pour over salad. Follow at once by drizzling honey over entire mixture, sprinkling with sunflower seeds. Lightly toss the salad.

Fourth of July/Independence Day Party

Does one or both of them realize having a baby means a modification of their independence? Is the baby due in July? Is the baby seeking independence from the confines of the womb? The coolest thing about holiday parties is that you can get cheap, cheap, cheap decorations if the holiday has already just passed for real. You know what to do—get some firecrackers, dress everything in red, white, and blue.

Obviously, the invitation will have to explain it's the Fourth of July in May or October and why. Do corn on the cob, hot dogs, brownies, and apple pie with ice cream—even if you have to do it inside because it's snowing!

Fourth of July Baby Shower Windsocks

You'll need:
Blue construction paper
Stapler
A manila file folder
Silver spray paint
Red and white crepe paper streamers (one roll of each)
Red yarn

Here's what to do:

Step 1: On newspaper, lay the blue construction paper flat. Cut star-shapes out of the manila folder and randomly place them on the construction paper. Lightly spray over them with the silver spray paint, so the star underneath stays blue but is framed by a bright silver cloud of paint. At least three stars per piece of paper is a good idea.

Step 2: Along one long edge of the construction paper, attach alternately red and white 10-inch-long pieces of streamers.

Step 3: Roll into a windsock shape and staple to seal. Staple red yarn hangers to the other side.

Eternal Secrets Crystal Ball

This is a funny idea for a shower, because it looks great on the table and everyone will want to know what the heck it is! You need to tell them that this is a real crystal ball, and that there are true fortunes inside. You can even comment about how California is a woo-woo state. Don't worry—we won't send any curses after you. We're proud of our varied culture!

You'll need:
4 envelopes of unflavored gelatin (clear kind)
4 c. of lemon-lime soda
A round stainless steel bowl
Pink and blue construction paper
Plastic wrap

Here's what to do:
1. Follow the instructions on making the gelatin, but use the soda to replace the water.
2. Pour into mold and refrigerate until it gets gooey, like an egg white.
3. While it's chilling, write fortunes on the strips of paper. Write a different fortune on each one, but on one, write "You will soon have a baby!"
4. Wrap each fortune tightly in a strip of plastic wrap (or they will bleed into the mold). Mark the one that says, "You will soon have a baby!" by folding it in a different manner than the others, or some other method obvious only to you. When you assist the guest of honor through the line, make sure you serve her the piece of gelatin that has her fortune on it.
5. Let the other guests serve themselves.

Recipe

The Most Amazing Shower Cake You'll Ever See!

This has got to be the coolest idea I've ever seen. I've adapted this from a book called *The Special Effects Cookbook,* by Michael Samonek. This is so amazing! I've modified it for the shower, but it's a doozy!

To make this unbelievable cake, you'll need:

1 box of confetti cake mix
1 tub of white frosting
A tube of pink frosting
3 balloons, one pink, one yellow and one blue
One helium-filled balloon
A long piece of thin wire
A package of "It's a Girl!" or "It's a Boy" confetti (which is not edible) from the party goods store, OR if you want it to be edible (so guests don't have to pick confetti out of their food), use regular candy sprinkles
A wire cake rack

Here's what you do:

1. Bake the cake into two 8 inch rounds.

2. Put them side by side on the wire rack, not stacked. Frost with white frosting and write "Welcome <Baby's Name>" or some similar shower message.

3. Take the three colored round balloons (not the helium one) and put about one cup in each of whatever cake decoration you've decided to use. (I like the confetti idea. Picking it out of the frosting is the admission price of this amazing trick!)

4. Now blow up the balloons and tie them closed.

5. Get the helium balloon filled with helium and tie it above the three filled balloons so that it holds them up. Use the wire to tie the entire ensemble, with the helium balloon on top and the three filled balloons below, to the wire rack directly between the two cakes.

6. When it's time, tell everyone to stand back. Have someone pop the balloons, causing them to explode, scattering their contents all over the shower cake. Doesn't that sound cool?

SPECIAL NOTE: I have never tried this, but you can bet I will for my next party.

Recipe

Lora Lewis's Most Amazing Brownies

You'll need:
2 eggs
1 c. sugar
½ c. butter
½ c. flour
⅓ c. cocoa
¼ t. salt
1 t. vanilla
½ c. nuts

Instructions:

1. Preheat oven to 350 degrees, grease a 9" x 9" x 2" pan.

2. Beat the eggs, add sugar and butter. Beat well.

3. Separately, stir together dry ingredients (flour, cocoa, salt).

4. Add dry to moist ingredients and stir thoroughly. Add vanilla.

5. Stir in the nuts and pour into the pan.

6. NOTE: These brownies will NOT test done! Bake for 25 minutes at 350 degrees.

Christmas in April/June/July . . . or Even December!

Baby's First Christmas—a little early! Theme your party around Christmas! Have everyone bring a Christmas ornament or some other carefully selected holiday decoration for the happy new parents. You could give Santa hats to everyone who shows up (which would make for great pictures). Why not hire the Stripping Santa (for the right crowd), serve eggnog, stack the presents in a sleigh you made out of cardboard, give the guests sugar cookies or gingerbread men as take-home gifts and decorate the halls with boughs of holly! If it snows at Christmas in your part of the world, have everyone wear bathing suits and Santa caps to your party in July!

Of course, your invitation will have to explain the apparently wrong season, if it is. This is a GREAT party if baby's arrival will preclude his or her new parents from partying this Christmas anyway!

Baby's First Christmas . . . Almost

You'll need:

Tiny pink plastic babies from the party goods store as many as people you'll be inviting)
One piece of red felt
Teensy little pompom balls (white) or you could use cotton
A roll of ⅛ inch red satin ribbon
Heavy weight white card stock
Silver glitter pen
Envelopes for same
Hot glue gun

Here's how to do it:

Step 1: Starting over one shoulder, dress the minibaby in red ribbon. Hold the ribbon halfway down the baby's back and wind it around one leg, then the other, then back up over the shoulder and around the middle. Affix with a drop of hot glue. Repeat as many times as there are invitations.

Recipe

Of course, serving caramel corn popcorn balls is a must, and in this case, you can dye them red or blue so they come out pink and blue. Try this easy recipe:

Baby Shower Popcorn Balls

You'll need:
20 c. popped popcorn (about 1 c. unpopped)
2 c. sugar
1 c. water
½ c. light corn syrup
1 t. vinegar
¼ t. salt
1 t. vanilla
Blue and red food coloring
Candy thermometer or glass of cool water

Instructions:
1. Pop the corn and remove any unpopped kernels.
2. Pile the popcorn in a large stainless steel bowl or in a 9" x 2" x 13" baking dish and place in the oven on low (275 degrees).
3. Lightly butter the sides of a 2-quart saucepan.
4. In it, combine half the water, sugar, corn syrup, vinegar, salt, and five drops of the red food coloring. Conserve the other half of the combined liquids for the blue batch.
5. Cook the liquids to the soft-crack stage (to 270 degrees), stirring constantly. "Soft crack" means when you pour a teaspoon of the liquid into the glass of cool water, it cracks softly. Or, monitor it to 270 degrees using the candy thermometer.
6. Remove from heat and immediately pour it over half of the warm popcorn.
7. Stir just until mixed lightly. Butter your hands (or wear plastic gloves) and shape into balls 3 inches in diameter. Makes just over a dozen balls.
8. Repeat the process with the blue food coloring.

Homemade Candy Canes

One taste and you'll never buy the mass-produced ones again!

You'll need:
2 c. sugar
1½ c. light corn syrup
1 c. water
½ t. peppermint extract
¼ t. red food coloring
A glass of cold water or a candy thermometer
2 buttered 8" square pans

Instructions:

1. Combine sugar, corn syrup, and water in a heavy saucepan. Bring to boil, stirring constantly, until sugar dissolves.

2. Cook without stirring until temperature reaches 260 degrees on your candy thermometer, or until a teaspoon of the syrup dropped into the water instantly forms a hard ball. This will take a while. Watch the pot.

3. Remove from heat and immediately stir in the peppermint extract.

4. Pour one half of the mixture into a buttered 8-inch square pan.

5. Quickly add red coloring to the remaining mixture and pour into another buttered 8-inch square pan.

6. Allow to cool. When it's cool enough to handle, remove from the pan and with a partner or by yourself, pull it until glossy. The easiest way to do this is with someone else. Pull from either end, and then fold, it back over and start again. Don't twist it. Just pull in long sheets, fold and pull again. You can do it yourself if you hang it over the edge of the counter.

7. Repeat for other color. Twist taffies together, barber pole fashion. Twist and draw the candy out into a rope. Cut off twisted sections into 18-inch-long pieces. Work these one piece at a time, until you achieve the desired thickness.

8. Cut into 6-inch pieces and bend to form a cane shape. Allow to cool and harden completely.

Step 2: Cut tiny red triangle "Santa hats" from the felt (they won't really open, they'll be flat). Attach the pompom or bit of cotton to the end with hot glue. Hot glue one to each baby's head.

Step 3: Attach, write, or print the party info on the cards. When dry, squiggle over the entire surface of the card lightly with the silver glitter pen. Hot glue the baby on, front facing out. (They'll fit in the envelopes better if you put the babies in the middle of the cards.)

How cute! Little Christmas babies!

Other Holiday Near the Birth

If there is any holiday at all that's your favorite or the mother-to-be's, why not re-create it for the shower? Nobody says we can have only one per year, and decorating for this holiday will be a snap! (Especially if the real one has recently passed!) Thanksgiving, Hanukkah, Kwanzaa, Easter, Lincoln's Birthday, there really isn't anything you cannot do! It will make it easy to decorate and theme, yes, but it could also be a great time for guests who will create fond new memories!

Baby Shower by Mail Party

If some/all of baby's family, friends and are far away, here's a cool idea! Have everyone out of town send a present along with a humorous or touching note or memory for the mother-to-be, particularly about when she was young, preferably a baby. Set yourself and a few local friends up to have the "unwrapping party." Decorate some place and take pictures to send to the folks back home of the mother-to-be opening everything. It'll mean the world to those who cannot attend, and the world to your mother-to-be.

You would want to send the actual "invitation to send a present" on a piece of sturdy brown cardboard on which you have pasted a smaller printed explanation of what you want them to send. To decorate this invitation, use a bit of jute or even dress it up with a bit of ribbon and a tiny fan-folded spray of baby gift wrap. Naturally, you will wrap these invitations, and a label pread-dressed with your name and address on it, in plain brown paper, slightly oversized, and tie it with jute or twine. Very clever, and it will get the message across. This will probably cost fifty-five cents each to send, however.

At the shower, have the mother-to-be or someone read aloud the written memories before opening the packages.

Pamper Yourself Shower

Here's where you and the other guests pamper yourselves at the shower. Have it around your pool, or at a day spa, where you can isolate for the day. Or, to keep costs down, hire a manicurist, a beauty consultant, even a Mary Kay specialist who can teach proper makeup application techniques. Set up a long table in your living room with mirrors and pots of colors and pretend you're all in high school again experimenting with makeup and different looks.

Or better yet, hire a masseur or two—preferably the buff, tanned, young type—to come give everyone a massage at the party! Let your guests wear sweats or bathrobes and just have a "Girls Day Off" time. It might be her last chance before baby is born to take care of herself so luxuriously! Send everyone home with a little bottle of bath oil.

Attach the invitations to little bottles of ninety-nine-cent nail polish. Or else get decorative plastic bags—like gift bags for kids' parties—and stuff them full of cotton balls. Insert a brightly colored invitation shaped like a hand or a foot into the center of the bag and seal it. Mail them in large envelopes.

Guests bring gifts of self-pampering for the mother-to-be—a gift certificate for a facial or manicure, a husk pillow, a terry-cloth robe, flannel jammies, a bottle or two of nail polish.

The typical slang comment to someone who's taken a day off is, "What did you do all day? Sit around eating bon-bons?" Who actually knows what a bon-bon is, beyond some kind of candy? Here is an ancient recipe I unearthed. Make them in pink, blue and yellow

Recipe

Sittin' Around All Day, Eating Bon-Bons

You'll know why after you try these!

You'll need:
2 c. flour
½ t. baking powder
½ t. salt
½ c. butter
½ c. sugar
1 egg
1 square unsweetened chocolate, melted
1 t. vanilla

To make the frosting:
You'll need:
3 c. powdered sugar
3 T. water
¼ t. peppermint extract
Red, blue, and yellow food coloring

Instructions:

1. Sift flour, powder, and salt together onto a sheet of wax paper.
2. Cream butter with sugar in a large bowl. Beat in egg, chocolate, and vanilla.
3. Stir in flour mixture, half at a time, to make a stiff dough.
4. Roll 1 tablespoon at a time in your buttered hands. Place 1 inch apart on lightly greased cookie sheets.
5. Bake at 350 degrees for about twelve minutes, or until firm. Remove to cool on wire rack. Cool completely.
6. Place the wire rack on top of the wax paper.
7. Combine the powdered sugar, water, and peppermint extract. Separate into two bowls. To one, add red food coloring and mix until pink. To the other, add blue. Beat until smooth.
8. If the frosting is too thick, add a tiny bit more water. You should be able to pour it easily over the cookies waiting on the wire rack.
9. You can create clever designs by using both the colors of frosting on each cookie. You can swirl the colors with a toothpick or add another color to them.
10. Enjoy! After all the work you've done for this party, you deserve to sit around eating bon-bons!

for the shower, and you and the girls can truly sit around eating bon-bons. You can even use the extras as take-home favors.

Baby Shower Candles

Here's a cute idea for either decorations or party favors from the shower.

You'll need:
Cardboard juice concentrate containers (as many as you want to make candles)
Pink, blue, and yellow crayons, unwrapped
Candle scent (available at the crafts shop)
A cheap aluminum saucepan you don't care about ruining (as you well may)
A length of cotton wick OR thin cotton twine (hardware store)
Table knives or silverware (it won't get damaged)
At least 8 oz. of paraffin wax per candle (hardware, grocery or hobby store)

Here's what to do:
Step 1: Melt one third of the paraffin wax in the pot over very low heat. WATCH that it doesn't burn. If it starts to smoke, the heat is too high. When it is nearly melted, add ALL your pink crayons to the mix and melt them in, too. Stir with wooden spoon until color is thorough. Add a few drops of candle scent.

Step 2: Meanwhile, cut 1 inch more wicking material than each juice container is deep and tape it onto a piece of silverware. Place one over each juice can so the wick drops vertically to the bottom of the juice can, supported by the cross-bar of the silverware resting across the top of the can.

Step 3: Slowly pour the melted pink wax into each juice can to fill to one third. The wicking should stay at the bottom of the juice can, but if not, poke it down at once with a stick. Allow to cool forty-five minutes to one hour, so that a rather sturdy but not brittle skin forms on the top of the wax.

Step 4: Repeat Step 1 but add your yellow crayons now, mixing thoroughly. Slowly pour it over the slightly cooled pink wax.

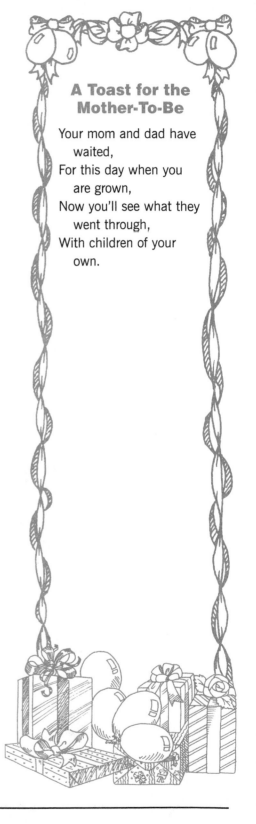

A Toast for the Mother-To-Be

Your mom and dad have waited,
For this day when you are grown,
Now you'll see what they went through,
With children of your own.

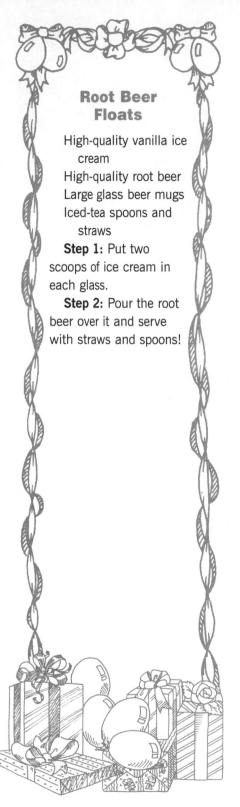

Root Beer Floats

High-quality vanilla ice cream
High-quality root beer
Large glass beer mugs
Iced-tea spoons and straws

Step 1: Put two scoops of ice cream in each glass.

Step 2: Pour the root beer over it and serve with straws and spoons!

Allow to form a thin skin before repeating the process with the blue wax.

Step 5: When you are filling with the blue wax, pour in less than a third, so that when you have completed the blue, you still have in your pot at least two tablespoons of blue wax per candle. Set aside.

Step 6: Allow the candles to cool enough so that a well forms around the upright wick. Then, reheat the remaining blue wax and slowly pour to fill the well to make the tops of the candles level. Allow all to cool overnight.

Step 7: Remove silverware, trim wicks to a reasonable length and then peel the cardboard juice tube from the outside of the candle. The candle will have a slightly waxy appearance, but you should have 3 rings of color.

Step 8: Take a very hot washcloth and vigorously rub the outside of all the candles to make them glossy. You're done! What an inventive gift you've made!

Cary Grant Special

What fun! Gather up the girls and load up on sappy old movies, root beer floats, and pizza! Give everyone a small package of tissues as a party favor. Pop the lenses out of cheap plastic sunglasses and make '60s cats-eye glasses by gluing some silver glitter to the outer edges of the frames.

Go on the Internet and download Cary's picture. Make copies of it, or one of his movie posters, and use them as covers on your invitations. This has NOTHING to do with babies, but EVERYTHING to do with enjoying free time before the baby is born.

Of course, if you're going to sit around watching TV, you must order pizza to go with the root beer floats. And what better way to follow up pizza than with something gooey and sweet. Sure, you can make a baby shower cake and all that, but how much do you and your friends really like cake?

Recipe

Try these yummy Peanut Butter Bars. They are very easy to make, and if you decorate them with a little plastic baby and some paraphernalia that goes with babies (rocking horses, pacifiers, etc.), she'll get the idea.

Peanut Butter Bars

You'll need:
1 c. crunchy peanut butter
2/3 c. butter (at room temperature)
1 t. vanilla
2 c. firmly packed brown sugar
3 eggs
1 c. flour
3/4 c. powdered sugar
2 t. water
1/4 c. semisweet chocolate pieces
1/4 c. peanut butter chips
1 t. vegetable shortening

Instructions:

1. Combine peanut butter, butter, and vanilla in a large bowl. Mix until well blended.

2. Add sugar, a little at a time, and beat until fluffy.

3. Beat in the eggs, also one at a time.

4. Stir in flour and salt, just until well blended. Spread in a greased 13" x 9" x 2" pan.

5. Bake at 350 degrees for thirty-five minutes. Remove pan to wire rack and let cool completely.

6. Combine sugar and water in a small bowl. Drizzle over still-warm cake in pan making a random pattern.

7. Melt chocolate with half the shortening in the microwave for a few seconds. Drizzle over the cake.

8. Melt the peanut butter chips with the rest of the shortening or a dab of butter and drizzle that over the cake.

9. Allow to cool, cut into bars. Pile on a platter. Decorate with baby stuff. You could do something cute and have little plastic babies climbing up the stack of cookie bars to reach the plastic bassinet at the top.

Ceramics Studio

(Or stained glass, knitting, or some other craft where the guests all take home their own handmade "souvenir.")

If you or the mother-to-be are into some interesting hobby, why not have the party at a studio? From there, guests can go eat in a local restaurant and open presents there. The object they create becomes their party favor. It could convert a lot more people to a craft or hobby your mother-to-be and you already enjoy together. This is an especially great idea if she's going to stay home after the baby is born and might need some encouragement to indulge in hobbies while baby sleeps. (They really do sleep a little, at least the first few weeks!)

If you are renting a place that commonly holds parties, they may provide invitations for you. Otherwise, why not send a colorful plastic paintbrush skewered through the front of an invitation shaped like an artist's palette for a painting class. Here's how to make it:

Paintbrush Invitations

You will need:

A collection of brightly colored plastic paintbrushes (the long, skinny kind for tiny touch-up jobs. They're often at the grocery store for $1.)

Lightweight white cardboard, tagboard, or manila file folders

Envelopes big enough to hold an entire paintbrush

A set of poster paints in primary colors

Step 1: Cut the tagboard, cardboard, or file folders in the shape of artists' palettes, not exceeding the length or width of the paintbrushes in any dimension.

Step 2: Affix the invitation details to the center of each.

Step 3: Paint a blotch of each color of paint around the palette. Allow to dry.

Step 4: Skewer the paintbrush through this and mail! C'est fantastique!

If you're going to do a party based on any other craft (one that will require no painting) you could send the least expensive tool for that craft along with the invitations to initiate people into it. For instance, let's say it's to be held at the arboretum and you'll be learning about which plants grow best in your area. Why not send your invitations stuffed inside a pair of gardening gloves, or tied to a small hand trowel? If it's to be a woodworking class, send a small, blank bit of wood (any will do—even from the local construction scrap site) along with the invitation. There are so many interesting ways to make this sort of party memorable, even for people who think they are all thumbs. Even in the worst-case scenario, it's going to be more fun than staring at her opening presents in your living room and acting amused for an hour and a half!

Ski Party

Right in your own backyard! She won't be skiing for a while, so why not let her do it one last time now? Wear big woolly sweaters, light a fire, and roast marshmallows, just like in the lodge. You'll serve hot chocolate, of course.

Get some knit fabric and cut tiny sweater shapes. Glue wood-grain paper or stick contact paper lightweight cardboard, and cut out skis. Hot glue first the skis then the sweater to the front of your invitations. Cute! Send your guests home with packets of hot chocolate mix you decorated. What do babies have to do with skiing? Absolutely nothing! That's why you're celebrating one last ski season before motherhood.

You could buy the baby a hand-knit ski sweater as a precious gift! Here's a great recipe for ski lodge canapés:

Nifty '50s Party

Let's go to the hop! Turn your kitchen into a do-it-yourself malt shop, complete with hamburgers. Remove your furniture and your shoes. Invite the guys—or don't invite them! Wear poodle skirts, hire a DJ, and have a dance! You provide neckerchiefs or bobby sox for the girls. Offer a bowl of fake tattoos for the young toughs; serve

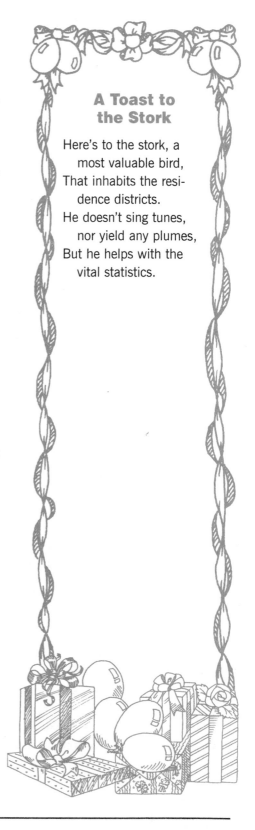

A Toast to the Stork

Here's to the stork, a most valuable bird,
That inhabits the residence districts.
He doesn't sing tunes, nor yield any plumes,
But he helps with the vital statistics.

Recipe

French Canapés

You'll need:
1c. flour
1½ c.whole milk
2 eggs
1 T. canola oil
2 T. sugar

Whisk together all ingredients until thoroughly blended.

Heat a 6-inch nonstick skillet, lightly greased (I use oil and butter together). When hot, remove pan from burner and pour in three tablespoon of batter, quickly moving the hot skillet so that the batter creates a thin pancake over the entire bottom of the pan.

Using a rubber spatula or egg turner, flip the crepe when the edges are bubbly to lightly brown the other side for a few seconds. Slip onto a plate, cover with a layer of wax paper or a paper towel (to prevent sticking), and process the next one.

(These may seem complicated to make, but they are as easy as pancakes and take less time to cook!) This recipe makes about twelve to fifteen crepes.

You'll also need:
Red grapes sliced in half
Smoked Gouda cheese, shredded
Minced onion

Step 1: Lay each crepe flat on a cookie sheet. Preheat oven to 300 degrees.

Step 2: Sprinkle half of each crepe with cheese, onion, and red grapes. Fold over.

Step 3: Bake for 15 minutes or until cheese is melted. Slice in wedges and serve at once.

If you're not a Gouda person, these are exquisite with a little chocolate sauce (melt a block of chocolate with a pinch of white sugar for texture) and a touch of Grand Marnier mixed in! Sprinkle with sugar if you do it this way.

bubble gum cigarettes. For great invitations, take a regular paper napkin and frill the edges out by scalloping them with scissors. On very cheap white paper, print out the party specifications. Insert it into the paper napkin you cut, and crinkle it like a waitress in a diner might have a crinkled handkerchief in her name pin in the '50s. Then, tie a knot with curling ribbon. Write the would-be guest's name on a piece of cardboard you might have even decorated, like the waitress's pin, and hot glue it to the knot in the curling ribbon.

Prego Poodle Skirt

She's the guest of honor, she's gotta look the part, right? Here's what you'll need:

A length of pink satin ribbon at least 6 feet long
Black felt
Pink fabric, about 3 yards, 54 inches wide
Sewing machine
A small "googly eyes" from the crafts shop
A tiny snip of red fabric
Hot glue gun

Here's how to do it.

Step 1: Iron a 2 inch hem along the entire selvage, and a 1 inch hem along the other selvage. Sew the 2 inch hem, leaving a small opening for the drawstring/ribbon closure. Insert the ribbon by folding over 1 inch of the end, attaching a large safety pin, and threading it through the entire selvage hem.

Step 2: Sew the 1 inch hem completely shut. This is now the bottom of the skirt.

Step 3: Cut a poodle shape from the black felt. Use the remaining ribbon to make a collar and leash. Curl the ribbon like a corkscrew and attach it three-dimensionally to the skirt by using dabs of glue just where the ribbon touches the skirt. Glue on the googly eye, a bit of red tongue, and a pink bow, and you've got a drawstring poodle skirt any pregnant woman will wear proudly . . . for at least one evening!

What to serve? Hamburgers, malted milkshakes, French fries—just like the old diners!

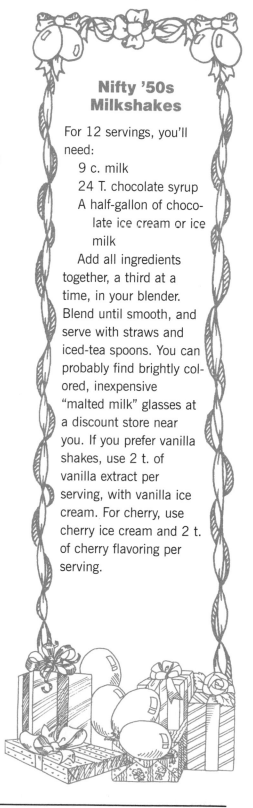

Nifty '50s Milkshakes

For 12 servings, you'll need:

9 c. milk
24 T. chocolate syrup
A half-gallon of chocolate ice cream or ice milk

Add all ingredients together, a third at a time, in your blender. Blend until smooth, and serve with straws and iced-tea spoons. You can probably find brightly colored, inexpensive "malted milk" glasses at a discount store near you. If you prefer vanilla shakes, use 2 t. of vanilla extract per serving, with vanilla ice cream. For cherry, use cherry ice cream and 2 t. of cherry flavoring per serving.

Slumber Party

When's the last time you went to a slumber party? Remember when you were little girls? Have you known the mother-to-be since you two really were having slumber parties? Make this the complete thing—with sleeping bags you rented, toenail polish, chocolate, candy apples, s'mores, popcorn, and ghost stories. Make invitations out of little pieces of fleece or fake fur you cut the size of hot dog buns, sewed together (quickly) inside out (fuzzy on inside, "outside" of the fabric forms the outside of the sleeping bag). Stick the long, oblong body-shaped paper invitations into the sleeping bags.

Remember: pregnant women may not enjoy sleeping on the floor in a sleeping bag, so provide an air mattress at least for her.

A slumber party is a great idea for lots of fun, but make sure she's up to it and willing to spend the night in someplace other than her own bed. You might want to plan it for a night her husband will be out of town anyway. Ostensibly, you can look after her while he's away!

Toga Party

Remember how much fun this was in college? A few simple bed sheets, some pins, and you're all set to party. You might like to invite the guys to this one. Make your guests wear laurel-leaf wreaths on their heads, just like Julius Caesar did. You can make them out of wire and leaves you buy at the crafts or silk flower store. For the mother-to-be and new daddy, spray paint them gold. Serve Greek food. Include some baklava with the cake, or send your guests home with some wrapped in pretty gold foil.

Great invitations can be made with some off-white linen paper stamped with a gold "Greek" border. You can probably find a rubber stamp with this pattern, or you can cut the shape out of a potato (in relief). Really, potatoes make good stamps, and you can surely get the gold ink at the stamp store in the mall.

Recipe

Caramel Apples

Medium-sized red apples, one per person
Caramel candies
Chopped peanuts
Wooden sticks
Wax paper

Here's how to make them:

Step 1: Wash the apples. Remove stems and place the apples on a wax paper–covered cookie sheet so they are not touching. Poke wooden sticks into their centers.

Step 2: Melt the caramels in a nonmetallic bowl in the microwave. Pour over the apples.

Step 3: Sprinkle at once with chopped peanuts. Allow to cool. Store in refrigerator. Do not make more than one day in advance.

Recipe

Slumber Party S'mores

Remember s'mores, that staple food item in every kid's summer camp diet? Well, just in case you didn't earn your Girl Scout badge in cooking, here's the recipe.

You'll need:
A box of graham crackers
A jar of crunchy peanut butter
A bag of good-quality chocolate morsels
A bag of large marshmallows
Aluminum foil and a fireplace OR an oven on low

Instructions

1. Smear the graham crackers with way too much peanut butter.

2. Sprinkle with way too many chocolate chips.

3. Squish a couple of big fat marshmallows between.

4. Wrap in foil and cook near heat for a few minutes. (If you're a real Girl Scout, they are bound to catch on fire. Mine always did!)

5. Or, place in the oven, not wrapped in foil, on a cookie sheet at 300 degrees for about five minutes, until they are gooey.

Book Party

Go to the local bookstore and find out which parenting authors are local. Call them or their agents and have an author come to read on the topic of their book. You might pay them a few bucks, or you might let them sell copies of their book at the party. Better, buy their book at a discount in advance from them or the bookstore (the discount from the publisher to you direct would be 40 percent or more). Let them read excerpts. Lots of authors have a great sense of humor and teach on their subject anyway, so you might want to investigate someone local who writes on what the mother-to-be is interested in. If you have The Learning Annex or a similar non accredited place that offers special interest night classes to adults, breeze through their catalog. Chances are excellent that just about anyone in one of those catalogs would jump at the chance to come over and entertain you and your guests for the evening. Terms negotiable.

Of course, perfect invitations if you invite an author would be bookmarks or book-shaped invitations that really open. Party favors could be $5 gift certificates to the local bookstore. (See the section on getting prizes donated in Chapter 11.)

Here's how to make a book-shaped invitation:

Book Invitations

Manila file folders
3 inch wide masking tape
Paying-your-bills-sized envelopes
Cordovan-colored shoe polish
Gold glitter paint in a thin tube (any will do: fabric paint, paper glitter glue, gold ink, etc.)
Old newspaper

Instructions:

(Makes four "books" at a time.)

1. Cut folder in half along seam. Fold each half in half lengthwise.
2. Using the size of the envelope as a guide, along the seam draw in pencil a book shape, curving up the corners for the optical illusion of depth.

3. Cut it out, but DO NOT CUT the seam! (This is how the book opens!) If you like what you got, use this one as your template for all the others. Cut them all out of the file folders.

4. Apply masking tape in strips to the outside of the book so that it covers the entire outside of the manila.

5. Place all of them face down on the newspaper. That is, place them all with the masking tape side up.

6. Apply some of the shoe polish to the backs of each one, covering the tape entirely. It will be darker each time you go over it.

7. Allow it to dry thoroughly (several hours). While it's drying, print out "pages" for the book by making a template for yourself with an area just slightly smaller than the book covers. You will need two sheets of paper for each one, the size of the whole book, so when they are folded in half in the middle, there are four pages in the book.

8. Write on these blank pages the party information, any prose you like (poetry?), information on the author who will be there, etc. On the last page, write "And they lived happily ever after. The End." (In order to get the right words on the right pages, remember that the front of one page is the back of the other when you fold them in half.)

9. Now that your covers are dry, write the word "Party" or "Baby Shower" or even "Angie's Shower" on them in gold ink. Allow plenty of time for drying.

10. Cut along the edges of the pages so they will fit, assemble them, staple them widthwise down the center, and fold them. Attach to the folded covers with a dab of hot glue.

11. Insert the books, when dry, into envelopes and mail!

What do you serve at a book party? A nice basket of different kinds of muffins and quick breads, a variety of cheeses, and perhaps some lovely fruit salad (see the Baby Carriage idea in Chapter 8) and maybe a wonderful salad. Here is the very best recipe I have for wonderfully sumptuous muffins.

Recipe

Scrumptious, Easy Whole Grain Muffins

These are line-up-around-the-block good. You'll use them for a lot more than the baby shower, I guarantee! I got the recipe for turning in enough box tops to the Quaker Oats company more than fifteen years ago.

You'll need:
¾ c. milk
¾ c. bran cereal
1 egg
¼ c. vegetable oil
¼ c. molasses or honey
¼ c. firmly packed brown sugar
1 c. Quaker Oats
⅔ c. whole wheat flour
1 T. baking powder
A pinch of salt

Instructions:
1. Combine milk and cereal in a bowl. Preheat oven to 400 degrees.

2. Add egg, oil, molasses, and brown sugar. Mix well.

3. Add combined remaining ingredients, mixing just until the dry ingredients are moistened.

4. Fill twelve paper-lined medium sized muffin cups. Bake about fifteen minutes. Serve warm.

'70s Again

Everyone dresses like the '70s and grooves to some slick tunes. Rent a 'fro wig or two to play with! Those ghastly clothes are everywhere now—you can get them cheap by mugging a local teenager. There are plenty of '70s composite music CDs around—you could buy them for the party and then give them away as party favors at the end. (That way, you wouldn't embarrass yourself by keeping them!)

Serve '70s canapés like Cheez Whiz, Moon Pies, Skippy peanut butter and jelly sandwiches on Wonder Bread, Cheetoes, Good & Plenty—all the tacky stuff you can remember. You can rent a mirrored ball for the tripping of the light fantastic at many party goods stores, or you can make one similar with aluminum foil wrapped around one of those big cheap plastic play balls for little kids you see at the grocery store.

For invitations you'll need:
A set of Tempera paints in primary colors
Poster board in a psychedelic color
A package of '70s themed stickers
Envelopes

1. Using the size of your envelopes as a guide, cut pieces of flat poster board slightly smaller so they'll fit into the envelopes.
2. Take some newsprint and spread out the pieces of poster board. Using your best artistic skills, paint peace signs or bold flowers outlined in blue all over the cover of your board.
3. After they've dried, flip them over and glue on party invitations you printed with your computer. Check your program—Microsoft Publisher has some '70s-ish icons to add. Attach with a few themed stickers, and put a few more on the envelopes before mailing.

Recipe

Dream Pie

Other than junk food, this is a delightfully delicious pie that will make a big hit. You can serve it instead of a baby shower cake if you'll decorate it with a baby thing, like a plastic baby or a little rattle or something.

You'll need:
1 9-inch round pie plate
1 package of Graham crackers
½ c. melted butter
2 T. brown sugar
1 container of frozen lemonade concentrate
1 9-oz. container of premade whipped topping
Half gallon of vanilla ice cream, softened slightly

Instructions:

1. Blend crackers three at a time in your blender, until they are crushed into coarse crumbs, but are not powdered. (You can also do this by rolling them with a rolling pin, but it takes more time.)

2. Add melted butter and brown sugar to Graham cracker crumbs and stir until moistened thoroughly.

3. Press Graham cracker mix firmly into the bottom of a pie pan (preferably deep dish).

4. In a large bowl, combine the lemonade concentrate, the whipped topping, and half the ice cream. Mix thoroughly with electric mixer.

5. Spoon into pie crust.

6. Chill at least six hours before serving.

7. Allow fifteen minutes of thaw time before serving, unless you are in a very hot climate.

Recipe

The Ultimate Elvis Cake

You'll need:

A white cake mix

A sheet cake pan (jelly roll)

Black string licorice (for hair)

Small silver candies (available at most specialty candy stores)

White frosting

Food coloring (each color)

A pair of cheap sunglasses with the lenses popped out

Instructions:

(You will be making a head and chest drawn on the blank sheet of cake.)

1. Bake the cake, baby. Thank you. Thank you very much.

2. When it's cool, remove it from the pan, wrap it, and stick it in the freezer.

3. About three hours before the party, remove the frozen cake and place it on a large platter or a board covered with aluminum foil.

4. Brush off the crumbs with a pastry brush, and then brush off the platter so no crumbs are evident.

5. Pile ¾ of the frosting on the cake in the center. Using the flat side of a butter knife, spread the frosting in every direction radiating from the center.

6. To make Elvis's profile, take a piece or two of black licorice and outline a nose, mouth, forehead, etc. (This is the only hard part—and it's not even that hard!)

7. Make a neck, and outline a white jacket with wide lapels with pieces of licorice.

8. Using the remaining licorice, form eyebrows, a nose, sideburns, and a mass of hair in a pompadour.

9. Mix a tiny bit of frosting with blue to form blue for his eyes; pale red for the lips.

10. Decorate his clothing with the metallic silver drops of candy.

11. If you're feeling creative, you could make a microphone with more licorice, or with a wad of aluminum foil.

12. Chill and serve.

Elvis Commemorative

Love me tender, baby! Watch one of his movies, play his songs, and even hire an impersonator—Lord knows there are enough of them! Maybe you could turn this into a dance? Would you serve food like in the '70s-themed party to commemorate the King's passion for quality food items? Award a pair of suede shoes, any size, you got at the thrift store and spray painted blue, to the winner of your dance contest. The party favors could be licorice records. Spray little plastic baby shoes first with Christmas flocking, then with blue paint, and attach little cards that say, "Thank you . . . Thank you very much!"

Elvis Invitations

For easy invitations, download his picture off the Internet, but I have a better idea. Buy ½ yard of white polyester fabric, some gaudy rhinestones and a studding machine (total cost under $10). Impress some rhinestones into the polyester, cut up the fabric into small pieces, and slip the pieces into sealed plastic bags. Attach a laser-printed note that says, "Genuine Piece of Elvis's Costume, circa 1968, Estimated Value $1200 — *Sotheby's.*" Send the sealed bags with a handwritten note allegedly from Elvis personally announcing that he's about to reappear just for the shower.

So what do you feed people at an Elvis party? What do you think? Peanut-butter-and-grape-jelly canapés, of course!

Elvis the Pelvis—
See the King Dance Live on Your Table

You'll need:

A blown-up picture of Elvis (off the Web? Photocopied from an album cover?) that is about 9" x 13" inches in size. A copy shop can do it for you, or you can draw it freehand if you're any good.

2 6-oz. packages of lemon Jell-O

2½ c. boiling water

A 9" x 13" x 2" cake pan

A cardboard box, approx. 10" x 12" x 4"

A clear plastic report cover

A disposable oval serving platter (like the aluminum ones they sell around Thanksgiving at the grocery store)

A tube of black or brown decorating gel

A can of whipping cream

Instructions:

1. Prepare Jell-O following directions on box. Pour into cake pan and chill until firm.
2. Cut open the back of the cardboard box so that you can easily put your hands under it from behind the serving table.
3. Place the platter on top of the box, and the image on top of the platter.
4. With a sharp knife, cut a 1½-inch slit through the platter and box right beside each hip. Remove the pattern/image.
5. Cut the report cover so you have a strip about 1 inch wide and 11 inches long.
6. Slide the strip over the image and through the slits cut into either side of the box.
7. Place the pattern/image over the hardened Jell-O and cut around the shape. Put the shape back on the platter.
8. Gently remove Jell-O with a spatula and transfer at once to the platter, covering both the image and the plastic strip.
9. Assuming it is still cold enough, you should now be able to test your work by pulling on Elvis's right hip strip through the back of the box to make him wiggle right, left to make him wiggle left.
10. If for some reason the Jell-O is too warm, it won't work. Simply chill the whole ensemble and try again.
11. Decorate around him, and his outfit if you wish, with the whipped cream. Make hair out of the gel. Elvis fans, control yourself!

Flower Party

Do it at your local arboretum, with a lecture on gardening. Have everyone bring a pottable perennial along with her gift. Give guests packets of seeds with little trowels as remembrances. Raffle off gardening gloves. Give a gift certificate to the local nursery, or have someone from the nursery come lecture on various plants that grow well in your area. Have guests wear flowers in their hair or wear dresses with flowers on them. Get plates and cups that have flowers on them. And serve salads out of big flowerpots you wash and give to the mother-to-be.

You could make paper flowers (see the Southwest Fiesta Shower) as favors, or make small topiary plants as follows:

You'll need:
Small clay pots
Dried moss
Dried roses on short stems (you can make them yourself by
    drying a bouquet upside down)
Hot glue
Florists' Styrofoam
A small sponge
Two colors of bright paint
Spray varnish (optional)

Instructions:
1. Turn the pots over and sponge-paint them with both colors. Allow drying.
2. Stuff pots with Styrofoam so that it is tightly wedged.
3. Fill in the cracks with Spanish moss, and glue it over the top so it covers the Styrofoam completely.
4. Poke three roses into the top of each flower pot so only the buds poke above the moss.
5. Spray varnish the whole thing. You're done! How cute!

Flower Power Salmon

Wonderful edible flowers make this a unique and tasty dish.

You'll need:
Nasturtium flowers, shredded
Violets, shredded (the edible kind!)
Squash blossoms, shredded
Fresh fennel grass
Lavender
Lemon grass, minced
Rosemary
(any or all of these flowers/plants will work)
New golden potatoes, peeled, about 1 per person
½ lb. unsalted butter
4 T. cream
Salmon, about 3 oz. per person

Instructions:
1. Peel, dice, and boil potatoes for about fifteen minutes in a large pot.
2. Place salmon on a wire rack set in a 13" x 9" x 2" baking dish with about ½ inch of water on the bottom.
3. Put salmon in oven for about twenty minutes at 350 degrees. Watch to prevent burning.
4. Mash cooling potatoes with butter and cream.
5. When fish is done, make a small mound of potatoes on each platter.
6. Top with 2–3 oz. of poached fish.
7. Drizzle with remaining butter and sprinkle with flowers.

Picnic in the Park

You can figure this one out all by yourself! Play old-fashioned picnic games and bring the kids if the mother-to-be has them, too. Give the guests red gingham fabric napkins, and buy the mother-to-be an awesome picnic basket as a gift. Have everyone bring a gift and a small nonperishable food item that they can picnic with. Send invitations written on red-and-white gingham paper plates.

Suggested Food Items:
Potato salad
Hot dogs
Hamburgers
Pickles
Watermelon
Grapes
Strawberries
Chips and dip
Soda
Lemonade
Oatmeal cookies (recipe follows)

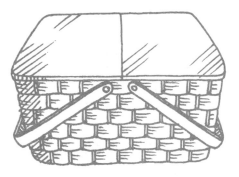

Chocoholics Party

From the plates to the food to dessert, do it with chocolate! If you want something done right, you have to do it with chocolate, right? If you don't already know how to make molded chocolate candies all by yourself go to the Wilton Cake Shop in your city, or at JC Penney's, and learn how. Plan a decadent cake, make sure someone brings the mom-to-be a gift of chocolate edible underwear and you're all set! You can get candy molds in baby-paraphernalia shapes and melt pink and blue chocolate candy melts into them.

Recipe

Granny's Extra Chewy Oatmeal Cookies

You'll need:
1½ c. flour
½ t. baking soda
2 t. cinnamon
1 egg
½ c. granulated sugar
½ c. brown sugar
½ c. melted shortening
½ c. melted butter
1½ T. molasses
¼ c. milk
1¾ c. whole rolled oats
1 c. raisins
1 c. chopped walnuts

Instructions:

1. Preheat oven to 350 degrees.

2. Mix the flour, baking soda, cinnamon, and a bit of salt together in a large bowl.

3. In a separate bowl, combine all moist ingredients and mix well.

4. Add all at once to dry ingredients, stirring until well blended.

5. Fold in nuts and raisins and oats.

6. Drop by teaspoons onto ungreased cookie sheets and bake until golden, which will be about twelve to fourteen minutes.

Recipe

Amazingly Decadent Chocolate Cake

You'll need:
3 c. flour
2 t. soda
1 t. salt
6 T. cocoa
2 c. sugar
1 egg
2 T. white vinegar
¾ c. salad oil
2 c. water
1 c. chocolate chips
1 c. chopped pecans (optional)

Instructions:

Preheat oven to 350 degrees.

1. Sift together the first five ingredients.

2. In another bowl, combine egg, vinegar, and oil and mix well.

3. Combine with dry ingredients and stir in thoroughly.

4. Add water and stir until completely mixed in.

5. Stir in chocolate chips (and if desired, chopped pecans).

6. Pour batter into ungreased 9" x 13" pan.

7. Bake forty-five minutes at 350 degrees, or until tests done.

8. When done, frost and decorate with the following items.

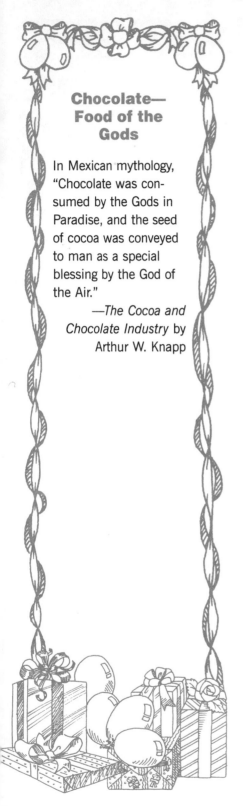

Aunt Rozie's Chocolate Frosting

Aunt Rozie, as we call her, is not my relative at all. She isn't even related to us, but her baking and my mother's instilled in me a lifelong love of the chemistry of flour and soda and the fragrance of freshly baked goods. Rose Neitzke was a victim of polio twenty years before the vaccination. She was sent to a special polio school in Chicago, where my grandmother's brother Bill attended, since he had (as family history told the story) contracted polio after falling on the ice while skating and breaking his hip as a boy. Uncle Bill and Rozie's eventual husband LeRoy grew up crippled but warm and loving people. Aunt Rozie and Uncle Bill were never able to have their own children, so they invested their energy in my family, their careers, and, for Rozie, her sewing and baking.

Aunt Rozie, with her leg braces and crutches, was a staple figure in my life as a child—the family scrapbook is filled with pictures of her holding first my father and then me as a child. Visiting her immaculate house was always a special treat—she'd slip me extra pieces of cake when my mother wasn't looking. The recipe above and this frosting recipe are from her. Too old to bake anymore, Rozie is the only survivor of the trio of friends who spent their lives trapped by a disease we thankfully no longer fear in America. Rozie is ninety-two now and lives in a retirement home in Chicago. So here's her frosting recipe for one of my favorite cakes, taken from one of the handwritten recipe cards she gave me as a wedding present.

Frost the cake with prepared "Dreamwhip" and chocolate pudding mix, if you wish, or you don't have to. It can also be done with simple whipped cream, or frosting, or just chocolate sprinkles. You will receive many compliments on this cake.

—All my love, Aunt Rozie

Recipe

Aunt Rozie's Chocolate Frosting

To make this frosting as Aunt Rozie really did it, you'll need

1 tub of whipped topping (frozen foods section of the grocery store)
1 little box of chocolate cake or pudding mix
6 crushed Oreo-style cookies

Mix together and spread on the cake immediately before serving. Mmmm. You'll love it!

How to make chocolate leaves:

1. From your yard, collect six large, firm, waxy nontoxic leaves. (I think magnolia is OK to use. I've used it before and no one died.)

2. Melt some sweetened baker's chocolate.

3. Wash the leaves and place them shiny side down on a cookie sheet.

4. Spray with nonstick cooking spray.

5. Pour melted chocolate into the leaves until full.

6. Chill them until ready to assemble.

How to make chocolate lace:

1. Melt some sweetened baker's chocolate or large chocolate bars (Hershey's works well).

2. While it's melting, line a jelly roll pan or cookie sheet with wax paper.

3. Take your colander (pasta strainer), lift it above the wax paper, and slowly pour the melted chocolate into the colander while moving it over the wax paper rapidly in long, fluid movements.

4. Chill and peel off wax paper to apply.

Recipe

World's Best Chocolate Truffles

You'll need:

8 oz. cream cheese, softened
5 oz. unsweetened dark chocolate, melted
4 c. powdered sugar
½ c. chopped dried Bing cherries
1 t. cherry liqueur or vanilla extract
3 c. semisweet chocolate chips
¼ c. shortening (real shortening, NOT butter, oil, or margarine)
A wire coat hanger
Extra cocoa
Shredded coconut (sweetened or unsweetened)

Instructions:

1. Slowly add the powdered sugar to the cream cheese, mixing well after each addition.
2. Add the chocolate, cherries, and liqueur (or vanilla)
3. Mix well and chill two hours.
4. Form these truffle centers into 1-inch balls when hard, and place on a wax paper–lined cookie sheet and put back into the fridge.
5. To make the coating, melt the chocolate pieces and the shortening in a glass bowl in the microwave and stir until smooth.
6. Meanwhile, bend the coat hanger into a hook on one end to form a hollow spoonlike shape.
7. Place a truffle center on the hook and lower it into the melted chocolate coating bowl.
8. Immediately sprinkle with coconut or roll in the extra cocoa.
9. Replace on wax paper and chill until served. Watch out! These are addictive. If you try one before serving, there may not be any left by the time the guests arrive.

Recipe

Chocolate Clouds *(Amazingly easy to make!)*

You'll need:

3 egg whites, at room temperature
⅛ t. c ream of tartar
¾ c. sugar
1 t. vanilla
2 T. cocoa
10 oz. semisweet chocolate chips

Instructions:

1. Heat oven to 300 degrees.
2. Place a large spotlessly clean bowl and your mixer's beaters in the fridge for ten minutes to chill.
3. Line cookie sheets with wax paper (or parchment paper if you have it).
4. In the clean bowl, add the egg whites and the cream of tartar and mix until soft peaks form.
5. Slowly add sugar and vanilla, beating after each addition. Beat until you achieve stiff peaks, sugar is dissolved, and the mixture is glossy and smooth-looking.
6. Gently sprinkle cocoa over surface of bowl and fold in carefully.
7. Fold in chocolate pieces and drop by heaping tablespoons onto the cookie sheets.
8. Bake thirty to forty-five minutes (you have to watch them) just until they are dry (in a meringue sort of way).
9. Carefully peel the cookies off the paper and cool completely on a wire rack.
10. Store in an airtight bowl until you are ready to serve.

Baby Quilting Bee

This is a charming, old-fashioned way to have a baby shower. You'd want to make sure most of the quilt was done before the shower, because you cannot do the whole thing in one evening. Set up a quilting bee of women who can or will use a needle properly. Give the result as a collective gift to the mother-to-be. You'll probably have to hire someone to design it, finish it, or start it before. Set the quilt out on a big table (ask at the fabric store how it's done properly) and have everyone bring their reading glasses and a thimble.

Adorable invitations would be to have a piece of fabric (preferably with a quilt print on it) skewered with a quilting needle. Spools of thread or a gift certificate from the fabric store would make a delightful shower favor.

Have each guest bring a quilt square she made at home to attach at the party, something special for the baby. Don't make it larger than a typical crib, however!

Here are quilt square-making instructions for you to offer to your guests:

Tell them to get one square of 8-inch" square solid-color cotton (or you can provide it for them).

Ask them to design a quilt square on a piece of paper, assuming a 1½-inch margin all around.

Then, with tacky glue (which is washable), hot glue (which will eventually come off), or the traditional way (needle and thread, by hand or machine), tell them to apply their fabric design to the square in preparation for the evening's entertainment, which will be (in part) assembling the quilt.

Invitations to the Baby Quilting Bee

To make a dozen, you'll need:

12 packages of needles (very inexpensive at fabric store)

A square of cloth per person if you are providing it, so it's all the same background color.

A book of discontinued wallpaper samples (get it free at the local interior design center)

Some brightly colored cardboard

Scissors

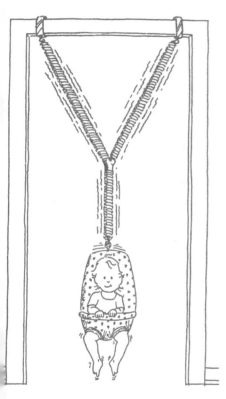

Instructions:

1. Tear out twenty-four sheets of wallpaper you like.
2. Fold the wallpaper in half lengthwise and cut out twenty-four different-colored pieces that are 5 inches wide by 7 inches long from the seam to the open end.
3. Cut them rounded at the open end. (They should look a little like tube socks, or a typical woman's breasts after she weans the baby!)
4. Make two equidistant cuts in the wallpaper, cutting through the seam toward the rounded end, about 5½ inches long.
5. Now, the fun part. Hold two mismatched pieces of wallpaper cutouts in your hands. One is the worker and one is the receiver. Open the first loop of the worker piece (either one, it doesn't matter) and weave it into the receiver. In other words, open the first loop of the worker and slide it over the first strip of the receiver, through the center loop of the receiver, and over the last strip of the receiver. (You never knew wallpaper was so flexible, did you?)
6. Now, for the second strip on the worker, slide it first through the first strip of the receiver, over the middle strip, and through the second.
7. Repeat Step 5 for the last loop. Now the two should be woven together in a heart-shaped paper cone that opens.
8. Repeat the steps for all twelve. You'll be amazed how fast this can be done after you've noticed the pattern.
9. Stuff the heart with the following: First, the quilt square, then the invitation—wedge-shaped and printed on pretty paper—and finally the package of needles. You're done!
10. If you want to get fancy, you can hole punch either side of the wallpaper woven heart and insert a piece of yarn or ribbon through each side, knotting on the outside, to make a little hanging decoration. Very clever!

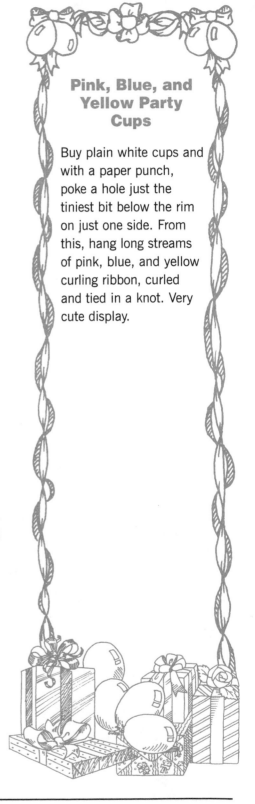

Pink, Blue, and Yellow Party Cups

Buy plain white cups and with a paper punch, poke a hole just the tiniest bit below the rim on just one side. From this, hang long streams of pink, blue, and yellow curling ribbon, curled and tied in a knot. Very cute display.

Housewife Party

What fun! If she's quitting work to stay home with the baby, do this fun party. Everybody wears fuzzy slippers, bathrobes or aprons, and hair rollers and mud masks! Get a more theatrical-minded guest to show up with a large pregnancy under her dress (a big balloon). Have your guests go home with a can of Ajax with a bow on top as a party favor. Award a pair of bunny slippers to the winner of your biggest contest. I don't think I'd invite the guys to this one. Give the mother-to-be a book on how to clean anything, and arrange a bouquet of feather dusters on the table. Have the mother-to-be sit in a special chair, from which she "rules" with her toilet bowl brush scepter. The greatest invitations would be rolled up, scroll-like and stuffed inside big pink plastic hair rollers tied with pink and blue ribbons.

I'd like to suggest that your gift for this shower be a Going to the Hospital Gift Basket.

Here's what you'll need:
1 large basket (preferably wicker)
Some wadded up newspaper
A baby's receiving blanket
A novel by her favorite author
A pair of warm socks in her size
Some wonderfully scented lotion
A great-smelling aromatherapy candle
A big bottle of water
Some snacks (her favorite kind)
Colored Cello-wrap (available in drug stores around holidays, crafts and gift stores all the time)
Some brightly colored ribbon (curling ribbon, fabric, other)

Instructions:
1. Wad up the newspaper in the bottom of the basket. (You could also use excelsior.)
2. Cover it with the receiving blanket.
3. Arrange the gift and food items in the basket. You may choose to tape them in place, or tie them with ribbon.
4. Spread two sheets of Cello-wrap on a flat table, one laid at 6 and 12 o'clock, one at 3 and 9. Each piece must be long

enough to cover the handle plus four inches when lifted over the basket.

5. Pull them up to cover the basket, tie with ribbon, tape the open edges with transparent tape. Voila!

Make-Them-Yourself Bunny Slippers

You could make a pair for everyone who attends, which would make a great party favor, or you could make them as a raffle prize, or as a special gift for the mother-to-be to wear during the shower.

You'll need:

A pair of pink terry cloth flat house slippers
A square of pink felt
A square of white felt
Four cotton balls
2 small pink buttons
4 large googly eyes (from the craft store)
Black yarn
Hot glue
A cheap plastic fork

Instructions:

1. Cut ear shapes from pink felt and inner ear shapes from white felt.
2. Glue inner ears to outer ears and allow to dry a few seconds. Hot glue to the tops of the slippers, saving room for the rest of the bunny's face.
3. Glue the two googly eyes in place, using black yarn for eyebrows or eyelashes if desired.
4. Break the plastic fork tines off and snap off the pointed ends to form blunt long white teeth. Glue onto lower part of slippers, but not so low the plastic teeth will catch on the wearer's socks.
5. Cut four to six long strips of "whiskers" out of black yarn.
6. Above the teeth, glue two cotton ball cheeks and a pink button nose.
7. How cute!

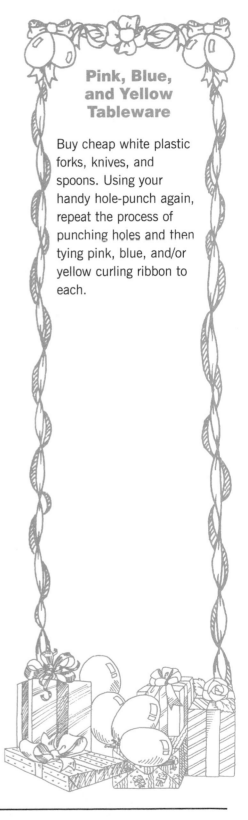

Pink, Blue, and Yellow Tableware

Buy cheap white plastic forks, knives, and spoons. Using your handy hole-punch again, repeat the process of punching holes and then tying pink, blue, and/or yellow curling ribbon to each.

Recipe

Simple Sushi

You'll need:
Fresh ginger
Some imitation crab meat, shredded
A tiny bit of mayonnaise, to make it all stick together
A little bit of lemon juice
Flat seaweed leaves (health food store if not at your local grocer's)
2 c. cooked sushi rice (same locations)
sesame seeds (toasted)

Instructions:

1. Grate the ginger finely. It is extremely potent, so use only a tiny bit.

2. Add it to the crab, mayo, and lemon juice.

3. Spread this mixture on the seaweed leaves and roll like a jellyroll, so it is 1 inch in circumference.

4. Slice the roll into ½-inch thick slices.

5. Place the warm sticky rice in a low pan and roll flat with a glass or rolling pin.

6. Sprinkle with sesame seeds

7. Cut into ½-inch wide strips.

8. Wrap rice around seaweed rolls. Chill and serve.

Japanese Party

Decorate your house in the traditional Japanese party style, with paper lanterns and cushions on the floor around a low table. Or hire a room at the local Japanese restaurant. Serve sushi, rice, and cashew chicken or snow peas, or just order in the food. Give everyone a pair of chopsticklike hair skewers. Have a kimono ready for the mother-to-be. Float lotus or even magnolia blooms in low dishes of water.

How very Zen of you to write your invitations on gray rice or vellum paper with a Japanese font or calligraphy or even a bit of brush painting. Or you could send them as origami.

May I recommend some simple sushi as one of your hors d'oeuvres? It is available in bulk at the grocery warehouse near me, but it might not be around your house. A quick recipe follows.

The Traditional Party

Just do the traditional thing—serve cake, coffee, and plenty of gossip and laughter. This is the most common type of shower, where you just hang out for a few hours with the girls. Nothing fancy is needed, it's very casual and it just sort of happens, without a real theme.

Surprise Parties!

A surprise party! What a wonderful idea! All you have to do is coordinate a time when your mother-to-be has absolutely nothing planned, keep at least fifteen people from leaking your secret to her, and figure out who should be invited, where the mom-to-be is registered for gifts, and what she wants most from the shower. Not that hard, is it?

In my experience, very few mothers-to-be (or for that matter, birthday girls or brides) are actually surprised by their shower. After all, they know they are having a baby or a birthday or getting married, and assuming basic social customs, they probably figure someone will throw them a shower.

Recipe

Petit Fours—Baby Shower Style

Here's what you'll need:
1 dozen small plastic babies from the party goods store
1 baked 13" x 9" x 2" yellow cake, cut into twelve squares and frozen
Petit Fours icing
One tube of stiff green frosting
One leaf tip (Wilton cake decorating)
A cake rack
Aluminum foil

Step 1: Line a lipped cookie sheet with aluminum foil and place the cake rack in the center. Put one-third of the frozen cake squares far enough apart that they don't touch on the rack.

Step 2: Drizzle with pink icing. Repeat with one-third of the cake squares for the blue and yellow icings. Allow to cool so they are firm to the touch.

Step 3: Make two or three green leaves with a leaf tip on top of each cake. Put the baby in the midst of the leaves. If you wish to, cover the baby's groin area with another leaf.

Step 4: Chill before serving.

Further, it really is tricky getting people not to talk about it to the guest of honor! Most people will be great at keeping the secret, but there's always one who apologetically says, "Linda, I'm so sorry I won't see you Thursday night! I have to . . . ." And then they see the surprised look on Linda's face (the same one she'll have to fake at the actual shower!) and say, "Well, I mean, I *had* been thinking we should get together for dinner some night before your baby and I'd kind of chosen this Thursday without telling you, and well, now I just cannot keep this dinner plan we actually never had" or some sorrier rendition of the same!

But if you absolutely insist on having a surprise shower, this section will help you handle it as flawlessly as possible.

First, your main objective is to get together a guest list that will include everyone she wants to invite. The easiest way to do this is to ask her best friends (if you aren't the best friend), the local girl-friends, or the new daddy. In fact, the absolutely best way is to ask each of them to come up with a list of twenty people they think should be invited, and then check for overlap and invite all the people on the lists.

Now, you have to figure out where she's registered for gifts. For this, Thank Heaven, you can ask her or her Mom (if you really want to be sneaky). Perfect! Make sure to include it in the invitations so the guests don't have to guess what the mother-to-be's tastes are.

Next step is finding a way to contact all these people. You are likely to get things as vague as "I know she has a friend named Jackie who works in the office next door to hers." Finding these people will require more than a little ingenuity on your part. But be persistent: you wouldn't want to leave out anyone who might be meaningful to the mom-to-be.

On the invitations, set the start time at half an hour before your mother-to-be is due to come. This way you ensure that even the stragglers aren't walking up the drive at the same time she is and thus ruining everything. You might want to say, "DEBBIE ARRIVES AT 7:30, SO PLEASE show up at 7!" on the invitations.

Once you have assembled a decent guest list, you need to take extra precautions to make sure no one who is invited to the party

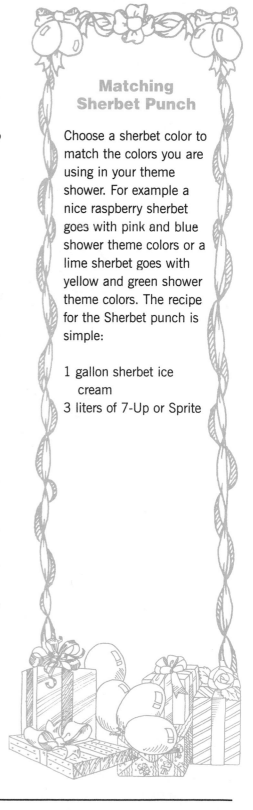

Matching Sherbet Punch

Choose a sherbet color to match the colors you are using in your theme shower. For example a nice raspberry sherbet goes with pink and blue shower theme colors or a lime sherbet goes with yellow and green shower theme colors. The recipe for the Sherbet punch is simple:

1 gallon sherbet ice cream
3 liters of 7-Up or Sprite

spills the beans. Mark the outside of the envelopes "TOP SECRET" in big red letters or write on the invitation "SSSSH! This is a surprise party!" You want to remind them on the map, etc., so that they will feel totally guilty if they screw up and ruin the surprise.

Make sure the mother-to-be can show up on the day you select. The easiest way to make this happen is to enlist the aid of someone she knows will NOT be throwing the shower to arrange a "date" with her the night of the shower. It is commonly the new daddy who acts as the decoy, but it could be another girlfriend or her mom. You simply get this person to ask her out to dinner on the day and at the time you want to hold the shower. Make sure the event she is invited to would require people to be dressed similarly to the way your shower guests will be dressed so that she is not uncomfortable. She should not be the only one prepared to go roller blading at your English Tea Garden party.

On the day of the shower, call the decoy an hour before the scheduled arrival, and ask if they are on schedule. Remember, the mother-to-be has a lot of details to handle, and she could be running a little late for myriad reasons. Make sure the guests park their cars away from the house. Tell the decoy to take a circuitous route to the location if it isn't a public or rented facility.

Turn out the lights, and be prepared to flick them on and swing open the door when she walks inside ahead of the decoy. Get the rest of the guests settled and ready to yell "surprise" as she walks into the room.

As hard as it sounds, the payoff is huge. Everyone who says that he or she hates surprise parties in truth loves the attention and the real message behind the party—that they are special enough to warrant all this extra effort.

CHAPTER 4:

How to Budget the Shower

Show Me the Money, Honey!

Now that you've decided on a theme, the next step is to set a budget. Throwing a shower is lots of fun until you start to total all the receipts. Then you find out that the extra $5 there and the extra ten cents each here somehow added up to more than you wanted to spend.

Then you'll feel bad because you put yourself in an uncomfortable financial position by spending more than you had allotted in your personal budget. You might find yourself begrudging all the work you did and money you spent.

If the idea of budgeting makes you queasy, or if you bought into the myth that "girls aren't as good with numbers," relax. Budgeting a shower is easy, and you can use the same principles to budget the rest of your life, if you are so inclined. As for "girls aren't good with numbers," bah-humbug! Just wait and see what a genius you are, using this simple system.

The first step is to decide how much money you can spend on this shower. Not about, but exactly. (Exactly makes it easier.) If money is no object, great. Make a budget anyway, so that it all comes out evenly and you know in advance what it will cost you. Refer to the section on party angels in Chapter 1 again if you must, but get your numbers straight today!

You already know you can save money by making things yourself. As you read through this book, you'll see many clever ways you can cut corners and still throw a nice party. You can also negotiate with the caterers, with the bakery, and with the rental location. You can get other people to bring things; you can get other people to send you checks. You can ask local businesses to contribute a coupon for dollars off certain services or goods, like meals, to provide you with raffle items or prizes for shower games. The only true limit on your wallet is your creativity. You can have the most wonderful party, if you are willing to supply a little elbow grease!

Now, if you're thinking, "How can I know how much I will spend if I don't know how much it will cost?" let me give you a few ballpark figures:

  ⚘ A cheap at-home shower without a meal will probably run you under $100.

  ⚘ An at-home shower with a simple meal will probably come in around $250.

  ⚘ A catered event at a restaurant with or without live music will probably cost you about $50 per person.

For example, let's take the cost of a shower I'd plan with food in my home for fifteen women in California, about $325. That works out to just over $20 a head. Here's how I would allocate the budget if I were planning the party.

First, write in the amount you have to spend on the first line. Then, going down the list, you will see the various things you can spend this money on. Spending more in one category obviously leaves you less for others.

Ask yourself and your cohost(s), "What's most important to us?" On the line provided before each item, rank the items in order of importance to you in pen. If it's more important to you to have great food than to rent a space, mark that first by putting a number 1 by it. If you really have to have live music, but you could care less about the decorations, mark that. There's no right or wrong; this is your shower, although you should try to think about the mother-to-be's preferences.

Now you'll have a great idea about what's important to you. If you wanted to spend all your money on just decorations, you could certainly find a way to do it! And would they ever be grand! But, of course, everyone would be starving. You are going to allocate some money for each of the items you marked as important to you.

You can probably guesstimate what the most expensive items will be, especially based on what you really want. So in pencil—and please use pencil!—write down how much you would like to esti-mate for each item. Start with your highest-priority item and work down your list in the order you ranked the items.

If the total of your list doesn't equal the number on top, your gross amount to spend, work it again until it does. Here's why: You can pay a bakery $40 for a shower cake, you can

Budget Planner

What I want to spend: $_____

	Estimated Cost	Actual Cost
Invitations:		
Postage:		
Number of guests:		
Rental space:		
Decorations:		
Flowers:		
Food:		
Cake:		
Drinks:		
Entertainment:		
Party favors:		
Party games:		
Present for mother-to-be:		
Music:		
Photography:		
Video recording:		
Cleanup afterward:		
Total:		

What I want to spend: $_____325_____

	Estimated Cost	Actual Cost
Invitations:	$5	$3 (made myself!)
Postage:	$4.80	$4.80
Number of guests:	15	14
Rental space:	$0	$0 (at home)
Decorations:	$60	$46 (found at discount shop)
Flowers:	$20	$22 (assembled myself)
Food:	$75	$78 (partially catered)
Cake:	$20	$14 (grocery store)
Drinks:	$10	$9 (mix from party store)
Entertainment:		
Party favors:	$10	$14
Party games:	$10	$6 (got raffle donation)
Present for mother-to-be:	$40	$52 (baby bouncer)
Music:	$14	$0
Photography:	$12	$12
Video recording:	$0	$0
Cleanup afterward:	$40	$38
Total:	$320.80	$298.80

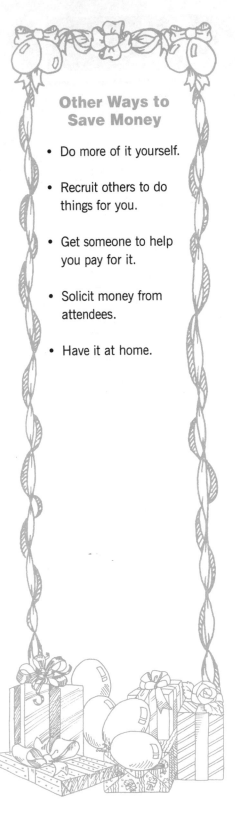

Other Ways to Save Money

- Do more of it yourself.

- Recruit others to do things for you.

- Get someone to help you pay for it.

- Solicit money from attendees.

- Have it at home.

pay $14 for it at the grocery store, you can do it yourself for about $6, or you can get someone to bake it, possibly for free. If cake is high on your priority list, $40 or $14 would be a good number, wouldn't it? But if cake is low, then free or $6 would be better. See how it works?

Every number you write down, you can find the same or similar things cheaper, or you can make them yourself. You can also find things that are more expensive. (It's just like life, isn't it?) Now make a copy of the list for each person on your delegation chart, and make sure she's told to stick to her budget or she has to pay for the difference herself. State that clearly now to prevent challenges in the future.

Once you have your numbers sorted out, you're all ready for the actual shopping. As you shop, some things will catch your eye, and you may readjust your priorities. Some things may cost more or less than you thought. Keep a running total of your actual expenses in the column at the right. Keep the receipts in a Ziploc plastic bag that is paper-clipped to your budget.

To be really, really precise about this, you could take the $325 in cash and place some of it in envelopes marked with the words "cake," "music," "cleanup," and so on. Then, when the time comes to pay for the item, you just open the envelope, pay the bill in cash, and put the change in a miscellaneous envelope. I know several people who run their household budgets this way.

Check out the following example of how I budgeted a sample party.

Budgeting your shower is easy. Remember, there are clever last-minute ways to save even more money than you thought possible.

CHAPTER 5

Choosing a Venue

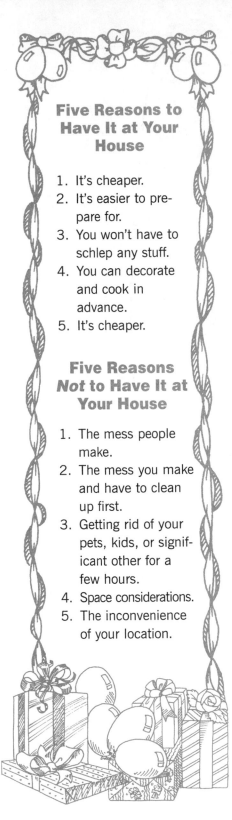

Five Reasons to Have It at Your House

1. It's cheaper.
2. It's easier to pre-pare for.
3. You won't have to schlep any stuff.
4. You can decorate and cook in advance.
5. It's cheaper.

Five Reasons *Not* to Have It at Your House

1. The mess people make.
2. The mess you make and have to clean up first.
3. Getting rid of your pets, kids, or significant other for a few hours.
4. Space considerations.
5. The inconvenience of your location.

Now that you know how much money you have to spend, when you want to have your shower, and it's probable theme, it's definitely time to think about where you'll hold it.

The Pros and Cons of Having It at Your House

Having it at your house gives you plenty of flexibility and saves you money. You have the benefit of not having to travel in addition to the other things you have to do as part of your shower duties. You can decorate your house and store food items any time you want, and it makes things generally easier the day of the party because you cannot possibly forget anything.

The main downside of hosting the shower at your house includes one heck of a mess to clean up when it is over. (Tip Number One—Hire a cleaning service for the day *after* the party. Doing it the day before is silly because no one can see the dirt once more than five people are in the house, anyway! Just hit it with some Windex and some Fantastik. Put away your laundry, and you're all set! But do hire a maid for the day after the party. Budget it in now!)

Another downside to having it at your place is it may limit the number of people you can invite. If you have pets, kids, or a spouse who isn't too into it, it may be a bother to get them out for the evening or even a few hours. You may not have room to invite everyone who would like to come. Your home may be in an inaccessible location, or far from the place most of the guests will be coming from (which drastically reduces attendance!).

You might not want to have the shower at your house for any of these reasons, and they are all good things to think of when you are deciding on the location. Location is often the biggest expense for an outside shower, so if you're on a shoestring, either do it at your house or get a collaborator with more square footage to help you throw it. One word of caution, though. Whoever's

Hostess Emergency Kit

Things to take if you're hosting the shower at a rented or unfamiliar location:

- Masking tape
- Scissors
- A box knife or a pocket knife
- Push pins or paneling nails (take a bunch)
- Duct tape
- Toothpicks (for rolling the tips of paper tablecloths before you nail them down so they don't blow off in the breeze, and myriad other purposes)
- Scotch tape
- A spool of coated wire with tin snips or some twist-tie wire (like from the produce department)
- A whisk broom and dust pan
- A roll of paper towels
- A bar of soap (maybe?)
- Bandages

- Aspirin
- Tampons
- Large paper clips (can be opened to form hooks for hanging things from the ceiling in rooms with ceiling tiles)
- Roll of toilet paper (maybe?)
- A cooler?
- Large trash bags
- Your makeup kit (because you will probably get sweaty setting up)
- Instant glue (in case someone breaks a nail, or more importantly, in case you have to fix something really quick)
- Three or four large preprinted signs that say "Debbie's Shower" and have a place you can draw an arrow
- A big black marker
- Any decorating items you plan to use

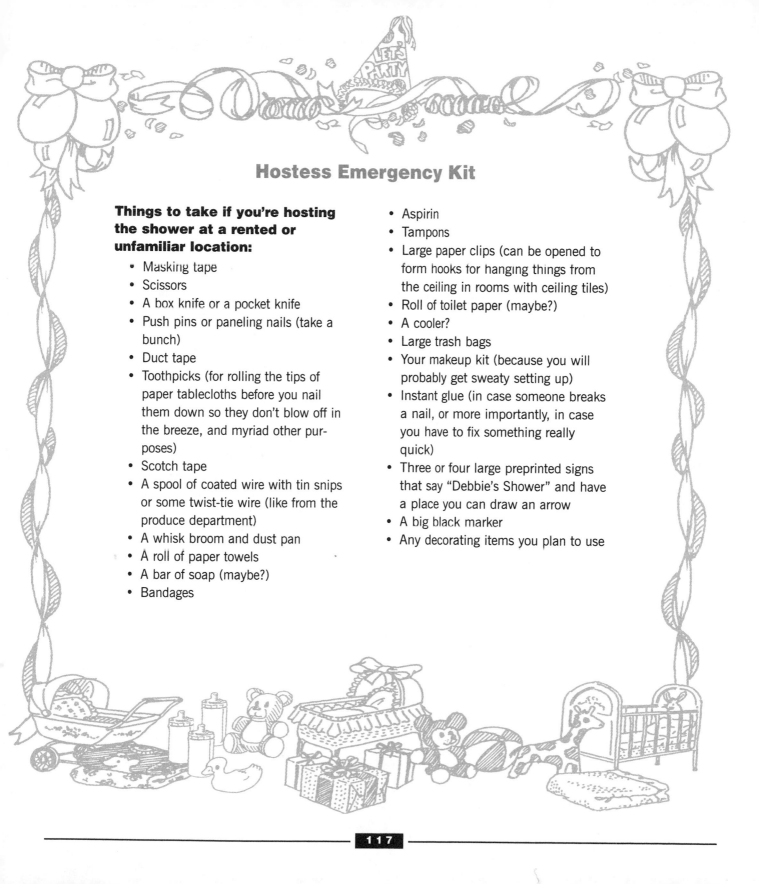

house it is at is the person who will be blamed or thanked for throwing the shower, no matter what the invitations say!

How to Find a Good Spot to Rent

Renting a location is a perfect option if (a) Your house is too small or inconvenient; (b) you can afford to pay someone else to handle all the crazy details; (c) you just don't want to handle all the crazy details; or (d) you simply prefer it this way.

Whatever your reasons, you will want to choose a rental space that has all the features you will require for your event. The place should be conveniently located and have plenty of good lighting in the parking lot, a bathroom, and comfortable seating. It should meet the criteria of your theme and general expectations. Is the gazebo fully shaded at 2 P.M. on Sundays? You will probably need to call and go look at several places before you find the right one for you. Look under "Rental" or "Hotels" in the Yellow Pages.

Some places will give you access to their kitchen and some will connect you with their caterer. Most will NOT allow you to bring in your own food or cooking supplies, so make sure you know precisely what you'll be allowed to do before you deposit any money.

Once you've decided on a place, ask the manager to set aside the date in writing, preferably in the form of a contract.

Basically, the contract should state the following things:

1. The date of the event
2. How long you will have the space for
3. What is included
4. Which room (by name) it is that you will be renting
5. How much you must pay
6. How much you must put down to hold the room
7. When the balance is due
8. What happens if you have to cancel

What happens if you have to cancel is especially important. You want to be sure that if *anything* happens—the baby is early, you decide to do the shower elsewhere, etc.—you can get some or all of your deposit money back. Most places will let you have some or all of it back up until a month before the event, and then the amount you'll get returned goes down.

Sometimes, an unscrupulous place will let you book a certain room, and then at the last minute, they will try to push you into another room that you didn't want. That's why you must get the name of the room in writing. Be a good businesswoman about this rental contract, and you'll be fine.

It's impossible for me to give you good estimates on how much a rental space will cost, because the factors that determine cost are region, space, demand, and condition. But you can use the sidebar on page 118 to check a facility.

CHAPTER 6:

The Guest List

Whom Do I Invite?

After you've chosen a theme, you probably have decided whether this will be women only, women and their kids (especially if this isn't the mom-to-be's first baby), or couples/families. Your invitations should clearly state "Children Welcome" or "Women Only" or whatever you've decided. Don't forget to include information on your theme, any special instructions, directions, what you want them to bring, etc., when you mail them!

Showers held at a club, office, or church have a built-in guest list, but call the mom-to-be's husband or mother and see if your shower is the only one that will be held. If it is, or for extra fun, why not invite her family and personal friends to your location? Wouldn't that be a surprise—to find her mother in her company's conference room at lunchtime!

Similarly, if you are the family and having the shower, or a group of friends, find out her supervisor's name at work and ask him or her what plans they have, if any. This supervisor could be incredibly helpful to you in figuring out who to invite from her office.

The best source of all is her husband. He's likely to know exactly who her friends are and who she'd like to share her baby shower with. He may provide you with phone numbers and addresses, too, which will be a big help and save you time spent playing private investigator.

It's better to invite too many people and risk being crowded than to overlook some people and hurt their feelings. You'll lose probably 20 percent of your people who RSVP anyway, so don't worry about it. Even if you are renting a location, if more people respond than you anticipated, you could always get a bigger space. But my guess is you'll be surprised how many people say they'll be there and don't show up.

If you're worried that some people will feel obligated and come when they didn't really want to, forget about that worry. Frankly, my experience indicates that people will make their own choices about whether or not they want to attend the shower. The birth of a baby is a happy time, so why not invite everyone who cares about the mother-to-be and see who shows up with an RSVP?

Do I Need to Invite Her Family to the Shower?

If you are not a family friend, and this is not the only shower, or this is just for co-workers or other people who are not expected to know the family, you probably don't. Ask the daddy-to-be if there will be another shower that her mom and other relatives will be attending. If there is, you need not worry about inviting them. If yours is the only shower, or if you personally are friends with the family, then certainly invite them.

However, if you invite her family, it is absolutely mandatory that you also invite the womenfolk from the new daddy's family, too!

About Inviting Men . . .

Sure, guys can come to showers. This is often fun for the new daddy-to-be, who might not be as involved in the whirl of prebaby celebrations as the mother-to-be. (Of course, he could be happy about this—you might want to ask him.) If you invite men, make sure you invite a few single guys if you have a few single girls coming, unless the whole thing is couples. (Try to find *cute* single guys—ask the new daddy for help! Many a match began with meeting at someone else's festivities.) If your shower includes men, it's best to have it in the evening or on Sunday. The shower category or theme, however, should be something of interest to the mother-to-be and the new daddy if he's going to be there. There are plenty of themes in Chapter 3 that talk about including men. Read through all the themes later and see if there are elements of some of them that you could combine with what you are planning. I'll bet you'll find things.

How Many People Should I Invite?

While I strongly believe you should invite everyone who would like to be invited, space considerations can be a factor. If your living room is 10 feet square with two sofas and a TV, and you have no outside space, you'll have a rough time squeezing in more than eight party-goers.

A typical at-home shower has about fifteen guests, plus the mother-to-be and you. Think about the location and time of day you'll be having it if you want to change from these norms.

In reality, if you invite twenty people, fifteen will probably show up, despite RSVPs assuring you that everyone will be there. A rule of thumb I always use is plan food for 20 percent more people than I invited, and plan seating for 20 percent less. Something always happens at the last minute.

When Do I Send the Invitations?

Mail the invitations so they arrive no less than two weeks before your shower's date. Ideally, you'll send them a month in advance. Figure it takes seven days for an invitation mailed first class to get across the country, four days for a neighboring state, and two days for a local address.

If you are inviting people from out of town to the shower, remember that airline reservations are much, much cheaper if they are made at least thirty days in advance, so work that into your schedule. I always find that six weeks' notice seems to cover all the bases.

Make sure the mother-to-be can make it, and if you are using an outside facility, make sure that you have confirmed your reservation with a deposit before you mail the invitations.

I Want to Do Something Unique with the Invitations.

Go back through the Themes section (Chapter 3) and read the many invitation ideas there. One for a theme other than the one you've chosen might spark a clever idea. Rifle through children's craft books at the bookstore. Look at an origami book to spark your creative self.

You can buy lovely stamps and paper for a fortune, or you can make them out of construction paper. You can laser-print invitations on paper you decorated or bought.

If the shower will be at work, you can make a three-dimensional invitation, like a paper flower on a stem, that you can just set on people's desks. You can tie it to a chocolate bar, or wrap it around a rock with a bow or a little plastic Kewpie doll.

If you have to mail them, as you will in most cases, you'll need to make sure that your art project will fit into standard-sized envelopes!

For a Hawaiian shower I once threw, I bought green, yellow, and red tissue paper. I pressed it flat and cut out flower shapes. Then I scored the petals so they had depth, stapled them, and covered the staple with a dollop of red paint mixed with glue. I sprinkled it with gold glitter and attached it to a sheet of ordinary computer paper that had the actual invitation information on it.

Ideas for cute invitations could come to you from the theme of your shower. I've included some suggestions in the themes themselves. People will be amused and delighted by your cleverness because so few adults take the time to personalize anything anymore. No matter how common or sophisticated your intended party, handmade invitations can make a huge impression and even attract people to your event.

You can find manila envelopes in 5" x 7", 9" x 12" and 10" x 13". You can get regular business-sized envelopes (#10s) in a variety of colors. Here, we have a place called Kelly Paper that sells wholesale stationery. You might have something like that around you. Before you invest a lot of energy in the invitations, I'd snoop around there. This month, I saw some really cute blue paper with pink and yellow ribbons on it that could have made very simple but nice invitations.

What Do I Include with the Invitations?

If you want to make your own life easier, you will definitely not forget to include these things with the invitation:

- Date, time, and length of the shower (that is, when you want them to arrive and leave)
- Whom guests may bring (kids, dogs, spouses or mates?)
- The name of the mother-to-be and the baby's name and/or gender if appropriate in advance
- A map to your house/the location (See the section "How Do I Make Sure They All Get to My House?" in this chapter—and follow the directions given exactly!)
- A description of the theme
- Appropriate gift selections for your theme
- An assigned type of dish if you are having a potluck (e.g., please bring a green salad that can serve ten people)
- If you are serving a meal or not, they need to know that
- What to wear, if necessary (e.g., everyone wears costumes, or semiformal, or swimsuits and jeans)
- RSVP information—MANDATORY if you are serving a meal or having one catered
- A deadline to respond to the RSVP

What Is an RSVP Anyway?

Here's a bit of trivia for any magpie word trivia buffs like myself. R.S.V.P. is an acronym for the French *Respondez, S'il Vous Plait*, which basically means, "please respond."

RSVP CHART

RSVP Deadline is:_____

Use this chart to help you determine exactly who will be attending your party.

Name	Phone No.	Coming	Not Coming	Call 1	Call 2
1.					
2.					
3.					
4.					
5.					
6.					
7.					
8.					
9.					
10.					
11.					
12.					
13.					
14.					
15.					
16.					
17.					
18.					
19.					
20.					
21.					
22.					

For reasons the same as yours, chic French hostesses got tired of not knowing at the last minute if Pierre the butler and the housemaids Yvette and Soignee should set the Limoges china for six in the small dining room, or for the full twenty-four in the banquet room. As soon as they started requesting an answer in advance, poof! The idea was hardly rocket science, but it made life so much more pleasant, that it spread like wildfire across the English Channel, and we English-speaking people have been using it ever since.

How Do I Track the RSVPs?

Being organized is the secret of successful events. I've catered dozens of parties of all sorts, and I guarantee, being organized is the most critical part of a flawless event at which you, the hostess, can have fun, too. Figuring out who will be there is very important—what will Pierre do with all that china and crystal at the last minute?

First, know that whatever responses you get, actual attendance will fluctuate by about 20 percent. Someone will get sick, but someone else will decide they can make it after all. Just accept it.

Here's how to handle your RSVPs. First, generate a list of those you invited. If you created the labels for the envelopes on a computer, this is easy. Give yourself a sheet of paper with six columns. (See page 127 for a sample. Heck, photocopy it and use it if you want!)

When good people call by your deadline to RSVP, make a check in the Coming or Not Coming column and GET THEIR PHONE NUMBERS right then. Call those who don't respond by the morning after your deadline. Get their numbers from the dad-to-be if you don't already have them. Call them twice. If they still don't respond, not only are they socially inept, they are highly unlikely to show up, so you can count them out. Don't waste any brain space on this.

When you call to follow up on an RSVP, here's what to say:

"Hi, I'm Janet Harding. I'm hosting Elaine Feldman's baby shower. Did you get the invitation?"

They answer, "Oh yeah! I meant to call you!"

You say, "I am wondering if you'll be able to make it. I'm confirming the food now, and I want to be able to count on you."

They answer. It's over.

Or, if you don't get them, leave a message like this:

"Hi, I'm Janet Harding. I'm hosting Elaine Feldman's baby shower. I sent you an invitation but I haven't heard back from you. I'm calling to follow up. Can you please call me back tonight before 11 P.M. at (310) 555-1212? Thanks so much! I know it's really important to Elaine that you be invited, and I'm trying to confirm the catering arrangements."

See how easy this is?

If you REALLY hate this idea, get one of the women who said they want to help you with the shower to do it for you. Just make sure they DO it.

OK, now if they don't follow up within a day or two of your message/conversation with a commitment, then call again three days after your first calls. ANYONE who doesn't respond is either out of town, sick or not interested (or just rude).

You're planning on a 20 percent change ratio anyway, but using this foolproof, proven method, you're bound to get most of your answers.

How Do I Make Sure They All Get to My House?

People tend to understand directions in one of three ways: visually, cartographically, and sensorily. Have you ever noticed that? Some people, particularly women, give directions by saying, "First, you'll pass a big red house with marguerite daisies in the front yard. Don't turn there. Go straight until you get to a Shell gas station, then turn right. You'll see a St. Bernard in the yard of the house on the

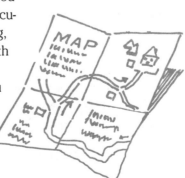

Bridal Shower Guests

mimi
grammy K.
Debbie
Betsy
Sarah
Skyler
Kelley
Helen
Janet
Ruth
gina

ann
Laureen
amy
aunt Judy
Kate
Theresa
aunt Reba
Samantha
nicole
Heather
Carolyn
Emma

corner, unless he's inside at the time . . . ." These are visual people. Unless you're one of them, their way of giving directions will drive you bananas! They know the names of none of the streets, but they know the colors of everything between points A and B. Personally, I want to strangle people who do this.

Then there are the junior cartographers. These people make me nervous, but where would we be without them? Columbus was a sensory direction person, but Amerigo Vespucci was the junior cartographer. These people tell you, "Head North on I-5 for 9.6 miles. Turn right at the second light on Old Creek Road. Continue West for 2.147 miles and my house is at 123 Dilapidated Barn Street." These people get places. I love them but am not amongst them.

Then there's the people like Columbus, and my dad, Larry. They find things by sensing where they might be. I still don't get how they do this. My dad is sort of like Columbus. Columbus just sort of bumped into America, although he was really headed somewhere else—India, I think. A little boo-boo, but all's well that ends well, right? My dad can drive into a city he's never seen before and sort of intuit where the hotel is, or where people he has never visited before might be living. Of course, you stay in a lot of hotels that didn't know you were coming, and meet lots of new friends this way by knocking on random front doors, but that's how some people drive to places. Those are the people who will look at the map you stuffed into the invitation, make a brief mental note of it, throw it away, and still probably show up on time. It's scary, but it works.

OK, so like Columbus and as my father's daughter, I guess I've meandered way off the point, which is that you should cover all three by including the following with your invitation: A small map (indicating North) that gives the route cartographically to your guests and a written set of instructions, such as:

If you are coming south on the 405, take Elliott exit. Go right. Pass the 76 station (on your right) to the next light, Waldorf Street. Go left 2 blocks, past the park . . .

If you are coming north on the 405, take Elliot exit. Go left . . . .

Use the visual cues (unless it will be pitch dark when the shower takes place and no one will *see* your visual cues) as well as written directions and an actual little map. Have someone else draw it if you're not good at it. There are Internet sites that will draw a map to your house for you.

This is really important because people tend to get flustered when they get lost, and it will not put them in the best mood for your shower. Your guests will be grateful for this bit of extra help, cued to the way they understand directions best. Further, you can double check it for accuracy and save yourself answering two or three phone calls from hopelessly lost guests frantic to get there in time on the day of the party!

What about the Gifts? How Do I Tell Guests to Bring Them?

Most people know that when they attend a shower, a gift is expected. Unless you are having a coed shower, it's American female lore to bring something to a baby shower. So you don't need to write anything specific UNLESS it's a themed shower, in which case you need to be as specific as your theme requires (for example, Winnie the Pooh, Feeding Baby items, boy baby clothes, etc.). It is expected and highly appropriate to tell shower guests about the location of the baby registry, if there is one. I think Toys "R" Us, Nordstrom, and Sears have them, among other places. This is where the mother-to-be has hopefully listed everything she wants from a specific store. That way, Brenda, who is flying in for the shower from Tulsa and who hasn't seen the mother-to-be since they were fourteen, will have an idea of what sort of things her friend is into now. You should list the location and contact information for the baby registry. Even if the guests don't buy something off the registry, it will give them a her sense of taste if they take the time to investigate. And if they don't, well, that's what returns are for.

Some Useful and Fun Gifts for the Baby-to-Be

- Baby hat
- Blanket
- Booties
- Bottles/nipples
- Crib mobile
- Cup
- Frame for photos or birth announcement
- Music box
- Silver rattle
- Stuffed doll
- Teddy bear

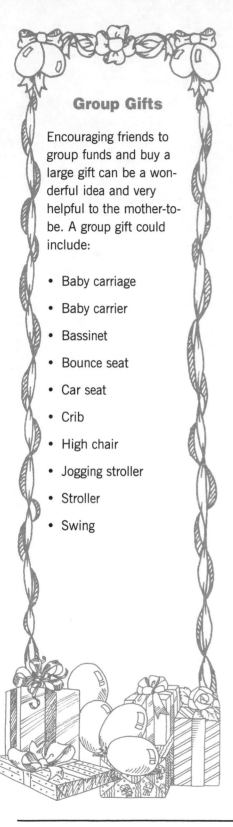

Group Gifts

Encouraging friends to group funds and buy a large gift can be a wonderful idea and very helpful to the mother-to-be. A group gift could include:

- Baby carriage
- Baby carrier
- Bassinet
- Bounce seat
- Car seat
- Crib
- High chair
- Jogging stroller
- Stroller
- Swing

Gift Suggestions

If she's the first one in your social group to have a baby, here are some things you might want to suggest as baby items. These things come from mother lore I've collected in the nearly thirteen years since I had my first child.

- Some babies come into the world already having outgrown the zero to three months size. My children arrived at (respectively) 9.12 pounds, 10 pounds even and the runt at 9.7. The average baby is about six to seven pounds which is newborn, zero to three clothes. At the end of the first month of life on the outside, most babies are wearing clothing that's three to six months size.

- Tell your guests to consider getting things in larger sizes based on the seasons. This way, your friend's new baby won't have thirty outfits for the first three months and nothing for later.

- Baby clothes generally come in preemie (for premature babies), zero to three months (which is quickly outgrown), three to six months (which is what most baby shower baby clothes come in for no apparent reason), six to nine months, and nine to twelve months. The reality is, most babies at three to six months of age will be in size six to nine. Figure out the season and buy appropriately.

- There are wonderful little cotton T-shirt things that she'll need a lot of. They are held together with snaps. Baby will go through two a day at least, so you cannot overbuy.

- Try to discourage people from buying decorations unless you know they are in alignment with what the mother-to-be wants.

- Gathering funds to buy a group gift like a baby swing or a crib is a wonderful idea. Just make sure she doesn't already have one.

- If it isn't her first baby, she probably already has many items from the first child. Some snooping around her nursery or asking what they've still got might answer most of your questions.

✄ If they don't have any baby stuff and you'd like to buy them nice but used stuff, remember this charming adage. It has a surprising ring of truth to it:

When your first baby drops its pacifier on the floor,
You sterilize it before putting it back in baby's mouth.
When your second baby drops its pacifier,
You wipe it off on your shirt before putting
it back in baby's mouth.
When your third baby drops its pacifier,
You let the dog retrieve it and put it back
in baby's mouth.

In other words, first babies, buy new. Later babies, it's OK to find nice used stuff (not clothes!) if that's all you can afford.

I Want to Make Sure All Her Best Friends Show Up. Any Ideas?

Getting the people most important to the mother-to-be to the shower is something you must think about when you set the date and time. Although surely everyone will try to rearrange their schedule to accommodate whatever time you select, if one or more of her closest friends will be out of town when you have decided to hold the shower, it's going to be sad. The easiest way to prevent this from happening is to decide who these people are and call them in advance—before you decide on a definite date! Make sure it works for them before you invite everyone else.

CHAPTER 7

Ringing the Dinner Bell

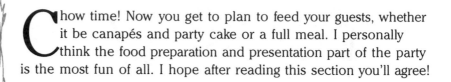

Chow time! Now you get to plan to feed your guests, whether it be canapés and party cake or a full meal. I personally think the food preparation and presentation part of the party is the most fun of all. I hope after reading this section you'll agree!

What Do I Feed These People?

If your guests will be there between 8 and 10 a.m., you'd better serve breakfast. If they're there between noon and 1, plan to serve them lunch (a cold cuts buffet is fine). If they are there after work, and it's for more than drinks, plan on feeding them dinner. If it's after the "American dinner hour" (which means after 7 p.m.), they will likely all have already eaten and only expect cake and beverages. Any other time, snacks are totally appropriate, and cake is expected.

Food for Thought

If you are hosting a shower for a friend who is kosher, vegetarian, vegan, or some other religious and/or dietetic discipline, it would be thoughtful of you to be considerate. Ask the mother-to-be or her husband, for instance, if she cares if you serve shrimp to the nonkosher guests, or red meat to the nonvegetarians. If a preponderance of your guests are of one dietetic persuasion or another, you would be wise to get some recipes from someone so you can cater it to everyone's liking.

Designing Your Menu

Take your time designing the menu for the shower. If you are planning to serve something more than cake and ice cream, you will need to plan out what you want so that your meal not only looks balanced but elegant, too. Your goal is to create the most wonderful dishes, probably with a minimum of expense. Planning ahead is what will make that happen.

Certain foods are associated with certain activities—peanuts and hot dogs at ball games, for instance. Your first step is to think about what foods mean something to you—which ones would fit in best with the theme of the party you are planning? If you are having a Hawaiian party, you would necessarily choose foods that have a Polynesian flair—things like sweet-and-sour meatballs with pineapple chunks, fruit punch, maybe pineapple upside-down cake. A lot of the themes in Chapter 3 talk about the types of food that would be most appropriate. Just remember that sometimes spicy stuff upsets pregnant women's stomachs, so have some mild food on hand, too.

Similarly, if the party is themed on a country or ethnic group, the food would probably be comfortably representative of that region. If you are not hiring a caterer, then you will most likely be doing it yourself with some help from your friends. You need to take control of the menu right from the start.

Once you have determined which type of cuisine you want, you are ready to consider the three most important items in buffet service:

Appearance, flavor, and variety

These three factors determine how nicely your food is arranged, how pretty it looks on the table, how good it all tastes, and how refreshing the choices are in their variety.

The easiest way to serve food for more than six guests is a buffet. I will assume you are planning to serve whatever you cook buffet style if you are reading this section. That's because a sit-down dinner in your home requires a lot of space and people to help serve the food. Buffet style, which means people line up at a food table to fill their own plates, is typical for these types of events. Specific notes for formal, sit-down dinners come later, as well as a brief section on barbecues.

Planning for Visual Variety on Your Buffet Table

Focus on "eye appeal" when you plan any party menu. Think of how the food will actually look when it is sitting on the buffet table or on someone's plate when you are choosing what you want to serve. You will definitely want an interesting variety of colors, tex-

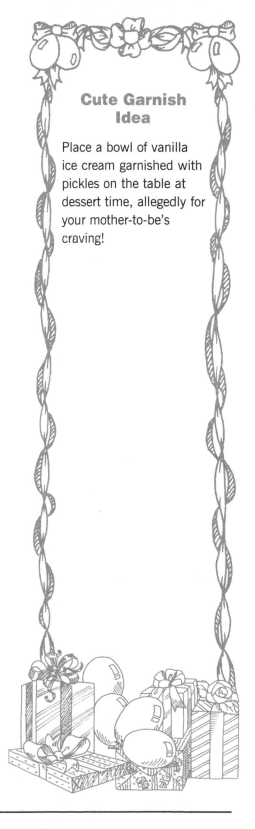

Cute Garnish Idea

Place a bowl of vanilla ice cream garnished with pickles on the table at dessert time, allegedly for your mother-to-be's craving!

tures, flavors, and sizes. Think about restaurants where you have really enjoyed the appearance of your food. What made it look pretty? The variety of colors (bright tomatoes, carrots, yellow squash, parsley, red or orange peppers) mixed with the entrée itself.

The visuals of food are simple. If you're cooking something, it's probably going to lose some of its original coloring. Plan to garnish it, serve it, display it, or accompany it with something else that is bright and colorful.

How Many Dishes Do I Need?

Choose no more than five major dishes for a buffet. That keeps everything much simpler and creates a more elegant appearance. Since you will likely not be hiring anyone to serve the guests as they pass through the line, having more of fewer dishes also motivates people to move through the line faster because they have fewer items to sample.

What Kinds of Food Should I Serve?

For a real meal, your dishes would most likely include the following:

One hot meat dish
One hot fish or poultry dish
A starch ranging from potatoes to pasta salad, rice, or rolls
A green salad
Some sort of vegetable dish, either hot or cold
And for dessert, the cake, possibly with ice cream and/or a fruit
    salad.

If a budget has you constricted so that you are planning the party at a nonmeal time, or if you simply want to keep it very simple, why not try something like the following hors d'oeuvres menu:

Crackers or interesting bread
One or two kinds of cheese (perhaps Brie and Colby)

An interesting fruit platter or fruit salad
A vegetable item (even as simple as carrot sticks and dip)
Some nuts or salty snack food like pretzels
The cake

How Much Do I Need to Feed Each of Them? How Much Food Does a Typical Woman Eat?

The typical American female eats precisely 7.0287 ounces of food at a baby shower, not counting the obligatory piece of cake minus the frosting, which she will leave in position on her plate. OK, I made that up.

Figure 1¹/₃ servings per woman. In my own mother's words, "It's better to have too much than to send your guests home hungry." The only time Mama is wrong is if you are hiring a caterer and it's costing you big bucks to be wrong. (But since you have carefully gotten your RSVPs back, you know precisely how many people to plan for.)

If you figure a serving is one hamburger, one chicken breast, one cup of pasta with sauce, etc., and you plan 1¹/₃ servings per person, you will hit it just about perfect. Which is, to guess that one-third of the people will have a second helping. I always consider any dinner a success if I have at least two servings left when the dishes return to the kitchen. (If there were only one serving, you'd figure someone was too polite to eat the last of it but was still hungry.)

If you are serving cold cuts or a buffet, you'd want to roughly calculate 3 ounces of meat per person and 1½ servings of bread.

If you are serving just canapés and deli plates with carrot sticks and other finger food, you can probably figure on about 1½ cups of food, loosely chopped, per person. That will give you a bit extra, but it's easy to figure. For instance, if you can fit one cut up taquito, a few nuts, three carrot sticks, and two cherry tomatoes into 1½ cups, you've got it about right. (P.S.—When serving finger foods, use six-inch plates,

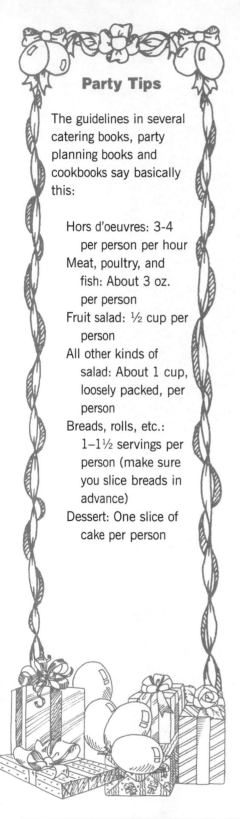

The guidelines in several catering books, party planning books and cookbooks say basically this:

Hors d'oeuvres: 3-4 per person per hour

Meat, poultry, and fish: About 3 oz. per person

Fruit salad: ½ cup per person

All other kinds of salad: About 1 cup, loosely packed, per person

Breads, rolls, etc.: 1–1½ servings per person (make sure you slice breads in advance)

Dessert: One slice of cake per person

not the big ones, which screw up your planning per person because people tend to waste more.)

People eat less in the summer and at certain times of day. If you've ever been to a buffet, you may have noticed that the cheap, bulky items are always put first, before the meats and expensive stuff. You can set up your line the same way—put the pasta and green and fruit salads at the beginning of the line and the meats later.

People, especially women, eat less in public than they might at home, so you can count on that, too. Nobody's likely to waddle away from your buffet with two full plates of chow.

For the cake, plan on everyone taking one piece and there still being a few slices left over.

For beverages, A general rule of thumb is two cups of liquids per person per hour. If we're talking alcohol, it changes, of course, depending on the potency. Two beers in an hour may be reasonable, but so would three ounces of a strong liqueur.

This isn't really rocket science, but sometimes cooking for a crowd can make you nervous about making sure you are providing enough. At the same time, you sure don't want to overcook and have to eat it as leftovers for the rest of the month! Use the above as a rough approximation. If you've invited fifteen women, twelve will likely show up. That's a dozen bread rolls, and you can buy one more package of six if you're worried.

Can I Do This Potluck?

Dreams come true! Everyone brings something and you don't have to worry! But don't take the huge risk of allowing people to choose for themselves what they want to bring! No! On the invitations, you must write clearly, "Please bring a green salad that will serve 10 people" or "Please bring 2 quarts of pineapple juice" or you will end up with twenty-five bags of chips at most parties!

If you are planning on having it potluck, you will need to be extremely specific in the invitations in requesting what it is you want your guests to bring. (See the section on invitations in Chapter 6.) You will need to determine precisely what you want and then be as specific as possible with your guests. You can even go so far as to send recipe cards and have guests make and bring the items on them. (This is not usually a way to win a popularity contest, however!) But it doesn't really matter. People who don't or cannot cook should be assigned easy things. Sometimes I forget that not everyone knows how to make even Jell-O, so try to be considerate.

The easiest way to get others to help you and not screw up your party's meal is to have everyone have an assignment and give everything a backup. In other words, you tell Jill to bring a green salad and Tonya to bring a green salad, too. The worst that can happen is you end up with two green salads. Otherwise, you can simply do it yourself.

Planning for Flavorful Variety on Your Buffet Table

To really be able to control how seasoned or sweet or salty the food is and what variety of foods you have on your table, you need to cook it yourself, cater it out, or have those who bring potluck do so from your recipe cards.

The idea is to provide a range of foods, prefer- ably things people don't get to eat every day, to make the party interesting. One easy way to do this is to grab a couple of gourmet cookbooks off the shelf and skim through them. Even if you are doing a really basic chili-and-cornbread hoedown shower, you could add variety by serving three different types of cornbread, one colored red or with pimentos inside.

Here's a place to assert your creativity. Try to choose foods that sound good, but don't be afraid to walk a little on the wild side. Pick things that you and your group wouldn't typically eat or buy. I remember the first time I ordered butternut squash ravioli in an Italian restaurant. I ordered it just because it sounded impos- sible. It was fabulous! But who would have ever thought to fill ravioli with mashed squash mixed with, of all things, cinnamon? It was wonderful.

I can remember very few of the restaurant meals I've eaten. But that one stands out. The same can be true for your party. Pick one or two items that sound unique from one of the gourmet cookbooks. Test the recipe in advance, of course, and you may find it's just the piece you need to complement your "usual food" buffet.

How Can I Feed These People Cheaply and Still Make It Look Nice?

So let's say the word "gourmet" doesn't work for you and your friends. Let's say the butternut squash ravioli story made you want to puke. OK. There are ways to get around this whole shower food thing and still pull off something decent.

In California, we have a wonderful place called "Smart&Final." This is a place where the restaurants go to get their bulk supplies. Check your Yellow Pages under "Restaurant Supplies." If that doesn't work, see if you can find a Price Club or a Costco or one of their many competitors nearby. It may well be worth the lack of service, long lines, and the price of a membership card to shop for the party there.

Buy the things you don't like to make. If you can shape hamburger patties but wouldn't get a kick out of making your own BBQ sauce, buy the sauce and save the money by buying the meat in bulk.

When you write your shopping list, write down the quantities you need of each item by using the provided measurements as rules of thumb. When you shop, decide where to cut corners to save yourself time. In general, buy higher-quality cheeses and meats and breads, and you can buy the less-expensive condiments and peripheral stuff. See the "Amazing Hostess" plan in the next section for food items you can prepare quickly and cheaply.

I Don't Have Much Time to Cook on the Day of the Party. Now What?

If you are running out of time or know you will be rushed the day of the party, buy some eternal favorites like potato chips and pretzels and dump them into pretty bowls. People love snack foods. And your job does not include serving things that would fit nicely into the food pyramid. This is a party, you can be liberal. It's OK to choose things that are prepackaged.

"You're an Amazing Hostess" Plan:

If you're really short on time and money, for a reasonable luncheon buffet follow this.

I'm figuring on fifteen women at the shower. Adjust if necessary.

1. Go to your local grocery store a few days early and see if they can put together a few platters of cut-up vegetables (carrots, celery, jicama, broccoli, etc.) with some sort of dip if the dip is included. (If it's extra, they have great ones in the dairy case.) Pick up the platters on the day of the party. Or buy the veggies loose, and wash, cut, and arrange them yourself.
2. If you have fifteen women coming, go buy yourself two or three bags of chips—corn chips, nacho chips, potato chips.
3. Buy a block of Velveeta cheese, a can of Mexican-style diced stewed tomatoes with onions, and two cans of refried beans.
4. Buy two ounces of different kinds of cold cuts for each woman. (That's thirty ounces, which is about two pounds).
5. Buy some presliced cheeses like provolone and mild cheddar, or get the deli guy to slice it for you.
6. Buy two or three different kinds of sandwich rolls to serve fifteen women, a jar of interesting mustard, and some basic mayo and American mustard.
7. Buy a head of Romaine lettuce, a bunch of parsley, an orange, and a lemon.
8. Go pick up the cake in the bakery department that you ordered two weeks ago.
9. Buy two cans of pineapple juice, two quarts of 7-Up, one can of Hawaiian punch.

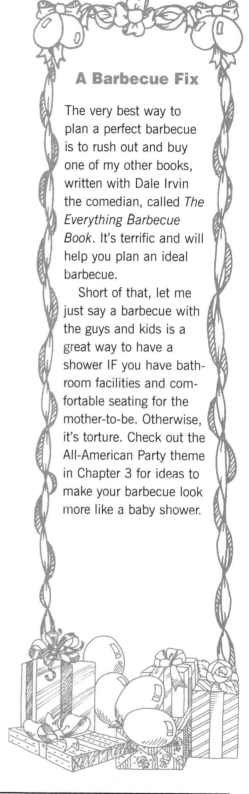

A Barbecue Fix

The very best way to plan a perfect barbecue is to rush out and buy one of my other books, written with Dale Irvin the comedian, called *The Everything Barbecue Book*. It's terrific and will help you plan an ideal barbecue.

Short of that, let me just say a barbecue with the guys and kids is a great way to have a shower IF you have bathroom facilities and comfortable seating for the mother-to-be. Otherwise, it's torture. Check out the All-American Party theme in Chapter 3 for ideas to make your barbecue look more like a baby shower.

10. Buy some paper napkins in pink and blue, and some nine-inch white plates and silverware and pink or blue paper cups. Buy a roll of each: pink and blue curling ribbon.

11. Go home and put it all together as follows:

The Do-It-Yourself 15 Step Shower Catering Plan

Step 1: Wash the vegetables if you are assembling the platters yourself. Slice, dice, cut, or chop as required.

Step 2: Get out two big platters or trays and two or three baskets. If you don't have a tray or platter, wrap aluminum foil around a big piece of wood or the side of a cardboard box.

Step 3: Chop up the Velveeta into chunks and place in a microwave-safe bowl. Dump in the beans and tomatoes, and microwave it for a few minutes until you can stir it smooth. Set it aside.

Step 4: Take the pink and blue paper napkins for the party and line the baskets with them.

Step 5: Slap the washed, dried lettuce leaves along the trays or platters, with the dark green parts along the edges and the white stalky parts all in the center.

Step 6: Lay the meats and cheeses in an attractive pattern on one platter. I'd probably alternate them. Garnish with parsley, two orange slices, and two lemon slices. Put on table.

Step 7: Dump the chips into lined basket, and arrange the bread in the other one or two.

Step 8: Put the Velveeta dip into a serving bowl. Stick a sprig of parsley into it and a lemon wedge. (It's good lukewarm, so don't freak out if it cools down!).

Step 9: With a rubber spatula, spoon the condiments into small glass bowls. Garnish with parsley.

Step 10: Unwrap the store-bought vegetable platters and put them on the table or arrange your chopped veggies on a platter around the veggie dip in a colorful fashion.

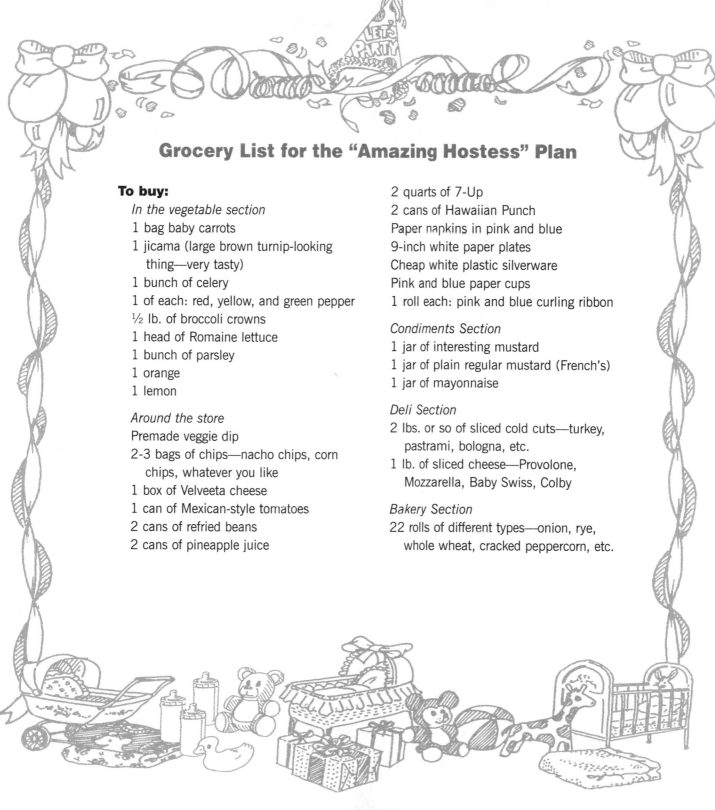

Grocery List for the "Amazing Hostess" Plan

To buy:

In the vegetable section
1 bag baby carrots
1 jicama (large brown turnip-looking thing—very tasty)
1 bunch of celery
1 of each: red, yellow, and green pepper
½ lb. of broccoli crowns
1 head of Romaine lettuce
1 bunch of parsley
1 orange
1 lemon

Around the store
Premade veggie dip
2-3 bags of chips—nacho chips, corn chips, whatever you like
1 box of Velveeta cheese
1 can of Mexican-style tomatoes
2 cans of refried beans
2 cans of pineapple juice

2 quarts of 7-Up
2 cans of Hawaiian Punch
Paper napkins in pink and blue
9-inch white paper plates
Cheap white plastic silverware
Pink and blue paper cups
1 roll each: pink and blue curling ribbon

Condiments Section
1 jar of interesting mustard
1 jar of plain regular mustard (French's)
1 jar of mayonnaise

Deli Section
2 lbs. or so of sliced cold cuts—turkey, pastrami, bologna, etc.
1 lb. of sliced cheese—Provolone, Mozzarella, Baby Swiss, Colby

Bakery Section
22 rolls of different types—onion, rye, whole wheat, cracked peppercorn, etc.

Step 11: In a big punch bowl, mix half of the beverage ingredients you bought. Add the floating ice ring (see recipe) and all the leftover citrus slices you can float on top.

Step 12: Put the cake and whatever other table decorations you want to use in a spot of honor on the table.

Step 13. Take a hole puncher and punch two holes in each paper plate. Take a 4–6-inch-long piece of pink curling ribbon and a piece of blue, and thread them through both holes and tie in a bow in front. Make the ribbon curl by pressing it between your thumb and a knife tightly and pulling it through to the end.

Step 14. Punch holes in the ends of all the plastic silverware. Tie pink and blue pieces of curling ribbon through each one.

Step 15. Arrange the paper goods and food on the table and relax! You've just catered it great!

Total estimated time (not including shopping or preordering): 2½ hours.

What Can I Prepare in Advance?

The day before, cut up the crudités (cold vegetables like carrots and celery). Wrap them in a damp paper towel and put them in a plastic bag, or float them in a jar of cold water in the fridge.

You can do any baking that will be necessary for the party. If you are making the cake yourself, definitely bake it the day before. Then, after it cools, brush off the crumbs with a pastry brush and slip it into a plastic bag. Store it in the freezer until three hours before the party. That way, it will be very easy to decorate.

You can wash and store any garnishes you intend to use—like lettuce, parsley, etc. You can make the rice and even the pasta if you add a little oil to keep it moist. Pasta salads should be made the day before to give the flavors time to meld.

Marinate your meat or tofu now. Chop vegetables to be grilled and seal them in plastic.

What Should I NOT Prepare in Advance?

Don't try to make in advance anything made with apples or bananas, like a fruit salad. (In fact, up to an hour before the guests get there, if you have to use an apple or banana for anything, dip the pieces in a solution of one cup of water and the juice of half a lemon.)

Do not slice any baked goods until a few hours before the party.

Unless you and your freezer understand each other extremely well, you should not attempt to create any frozen desserts, like an ice cream pie or whipped cream for strawberry shortcake, more than a day prior to the event. The temperature is almost never right when you go to serve it.

Don't mix the punch or add ice to anything until the moments before the guests arrive.

Don't get all mayonnaise-d out before the shower and end up giving people salmonella. Keep anything with mayo in the fridge until the last minute.

How Do I Make a Shower Cake Easily and Fast?

It's a lot of fun to make and decorate your own cake, and cheaper, too. If easy is called for, get a cake mix in chocolate or vanilla. If you get chocolate, add a half cup of chocolate chips to the mix right before you pour it into the pan. If you use vanilla, throw in one cup of frozen raspberries or raisins or diced canned peaches.

For the filling, try pudding or jam instead of the frosting that you can buy premade. I always make my own frosting, but if you don't want to, those little tubs of it from the grocery store work great. Figure it will take two of them to neatly cover a 9-inch layer cake.

Freeze the cake when it's cooled from the oven (the day before the shower). Then, while it's still frozen, brush off any crumbs with a pastry brush. Frost it while it's thawing. (It takes about three hours to thaw if it's not assembled. Frost it cold, especially if it's hot in your house!) Smear frosting on it with the flat side of a table knife. Work from the top down—dump lots of frosting on the top and smooth it over the edges. Once it's over the edges, pull it down on the cake and wrap around. Go over it until smooth. NEVER let your knife touch the cake—only the frosting—or you'll get crumbs in the frosting.

With a few metal spatulas, lift the cake onto a clean plate for final decorating. (That's how I do it—my cake-decorating teacher had much more fancy ideas about using wax-paper rings before you ice it.)

But I Don't Want to Get That Fancy! I Think I Just Want "Easy"

If you don't want to experiment with loops and scallops, even though they are VERY easy to do and SO pretty (urge, urge), just smooth out the icing as best you can. Sprinkle it with something interesting like pink and blue candies, little pastel Sweetart pacifiers (very appropriate), or candy beads. Be creative! Write "Welcome Baby!" across the top with icing and finish with whatever plastic thing you bought to put on the cake

How Do I Buy a Shower Cake?

If I failed to sell you on how fun it will be to make the cake, or if you simply don't have the time or the inclination to learn, you can always buy something nice. Here's how to do it.

Call four local bakeries, including the one at your local grocery store, to find one that promises you the best shower cake. Drop by to look at their pictures of cakes they've made. Taste something they've baked. If it has that weird lard aftertaste, skip them.

Recipe

Tools for Making a Shower Cake

What you'll need to make a shower cake:

1 box of cake mix
2 tubs of frosting (get white and a set of food coloring if they don't
    have frosting the color you want)
1 box of powdered sugar
2 layer pans for cakes
About ½ cup of flour, for flouring the pans
A bit of butter or some non-stick cooking spray
A butter knife
A serving plate
Some kind of sprinkles or chocolate kisses or something
A tube of decorating gel
A plastic ornament tied to the shower's theme (a bassinet, a
    sleeping baby, etc. There are hundreds of choices at party goods
    stores)
AND if you're going a bit fancier (and please do—it's fun!):
Two cake decorating/frosting bags
One tip with a small round hole in it about the diameter of a Q-tip rod
One tip with a multipointed star shape on the end
An extra container of frosting in a contrasting color
A gasket attachment to hold the tips to the pastry/frosting/decorating
    bag

Decorating the Shower Cake

If you're adventurous in the kitchen, you probably already know how to use a pastry bag to decorate your cake with scallops and loops. If not, here goes:

Use stiff frosting in a pastry bag with a decorating tip. (You can buy these cheaply at most places that carry party goods.) Stuff frosting into the bag by cuffing the bag open in half over your hand while holding the tip. Use a knife to scrape the frosting into the bag. Do not fill beyond half.

Now, uncuff the sides. The frosting will be in the front part of the bag, and the pastry bag will be clean and empty on the top half. Hold the top of the bag with both hands and tap the tip lightly on the counter a few times. Gently squeeze it to remove any air, which will screw up your frosting application.

Beginning at the very top of the frosting inside, twist the bag tightly to form a seal. (It now looks like a goat udder.) The way to make this even and well done is to keep pressure on the twisted part to make the frosting come out evenly. Just like toothpaste, don't squeeze from the middle! With your writing hand, you will guide the tube, and with the other, you will slowly squeeze down from the twisted closure to force the frosting out evenly and cleanly.

First, practice on an overturned bowl or drinking glass. Make a dab of frosting along the top. Then, keeping pressure even, pull away with consistent pressure and allow the frosting to fall slightly while you reattach with another dab an inch or two away. Practice it a few times; it's really quite easy.

When you feel confident, apply it to your cake. No worries that you have messed things up if a loop breaks. (It broke because your icing was too stiff or your pressure was uneven.) Just flip it off with a knife and continue.

When you find a design you like and a price that fits your budget, order the cake. Expect to put down 50 percent of the final price. Some places will deliver it to your shower location—wouldn't that be nice? Imagine the hassle of turning a corner while driving with the cake in your car!

You should order the cake at least one week in advance, and you should know when you order it how many people you will want it to serve. A basic round layer cake serves eight to ten people. An $11 \times 9 \times 2$ sheet cake (the proper term for flat cakes) will service fifteen people fairly easily. Don't let the baker talk you into ordering too much cake.

Is Alcohol Appropriate? Is It Required?

Serving alcohol is never required, but it is mandatory you provide nonalcoholic beverages if you are serving liquor. It's also a nice touch to have a pitcher of water with a floating lemon slice in it on the table. But as for alcohol, unless you'd like to spend the big bucks, it's far easier to spike the punch than to provide beer or wine or champagne for the whole crew.

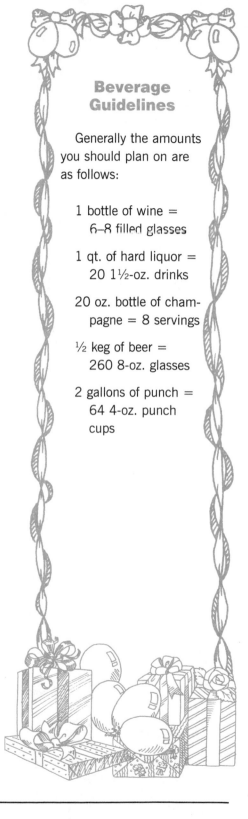

Beverage Guidelines

Generally the amounts you should plan on are as follows:

1 bottle of wine = 6–8 filled glasses

1 qt. of hard liquor = 20 1½-oz. drinks

20 oz. bottle of champagne = 8 servings

½ keg of beer = 260 8-oz. glasses

2 gallons of punch = 64 4-oz. punch cups

Although most baby showers feature nonalcoholic beverages, you might choose to add some alcoholic ones to your party. The only rules about alcohol at parties is that the hostess also provides nonalcoholic beverages and that she watches for overconsumption and takes appropriate measures to avert disaster.

Many cookbooks offer splendid recipes for alcoholic punches, which are the easiest and cheapest way to serve alcohol, usually. For a party of all women, you would likely choose a light, fruity alcoholic punch.

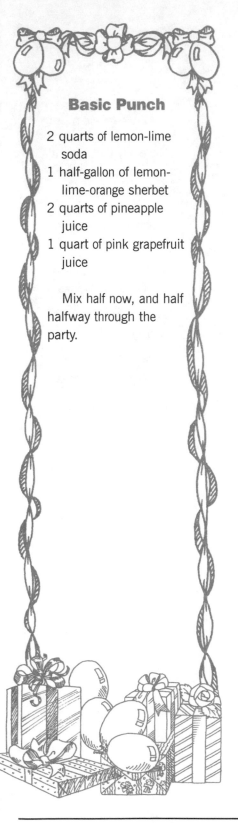

Basic Punch

2 quarts of lemon-lime
   soda
1 half-gallon of lemon-
   lime-orange sherbet
2 quarts of pineapple
   juice
1 quart of pink grapefruit
   juice

   Mix half now, and half
halfway through the
party.

Nonalcoholic Drinks

As more and more people become health conscious, fewer and fewer drink alcohol, especially pregnant women. Either way, a good hostess always provides at least some nonalcoholic drinks. The obvious basics are coffee, hot and/or iced tea, and cool water, preferably with a few floating lemon wedges. Other beverages to consider include:

> Lemonade (see the All-American Party theme in
>   Chapter 3 for pink, yellow, and blue
>   lemonade!)
> Fruit punch
> Sparkling apple juice
> Bottled water
> Soft drinks
> Fruit juice
> Vegetable juice

   You'd probably serve any of the above with a few lemon or lime wedges available, or set a punch bowl filled with cans or bottles and ice on the table.

   Of course, the traditional drink at baby showers is fruit punch, usually with sherbet floating on top

How to Serve Beverages

Drinks should be served at their intended temperature—coffee should be hot, melted ice cubes should not dilute ice tea, and champagne should be chilled. A lovely idea for a floating ice bouquet follows. It will stay solid for at least an hour and avoid diluting your drinks.

How to Make Floating Ice Bouquets

   Choose two or three cheap plastic containers, like the kind frozen whipped topping comes in. You can also use one or more Jell-O molds. Don't use Tupperware or some other sturdy plastic product, because you'll never get the ice bouquet out when it's frozen.

Fill each container three-quarters full with water, and float a few nontoxic flowers in it. They'll probably come to the surface. That's OK. If you want, tint the water to match your party décor. You can use polyester flowers, too, but use big ones so they cannot be swallowed.

Freeze solid and float in your punch bowl upside down when it's party time. They're lovely!

Remove soggy flowers and replace with backup frozen bouquets.

About Catered Events . . .

Catering is a wonderful idea but very expensive. If you are catering the event, you will have X dollars to feed X people, and that's it. If you want someone to cater it in your home, be prepared to pay a premium. If you want to have it at an establishment that offers catering, talk to the catering manager there. Be advised that few places that offer catering will allow you to bring in food from the outside, so check first before you decide to cut corners and bring in a cake from the local bakery instead of theirs.

If you are hiring a catering company to come to your house, speak to several of them before you make up your mind. Try to get recommendations of good caterers from friends. Also, read the tips for catering the party yourself, earlier in this chapter. People aren't coming because you are a gourmet, they're coming because they love the mother-to-be.

An average catered meal will run you between $17–$32 per person, rule of thumb. The nice thing: They do the dishes!

5 Steps to a Flawless Catered Event

Step 1: If you are using a rented space, confirm that they allow outside caterers, if there are kitchen facilities at the site and if you may use them, who is responsible if something breaks, what they provide, and so forth. They may have their own or preferred caterers.

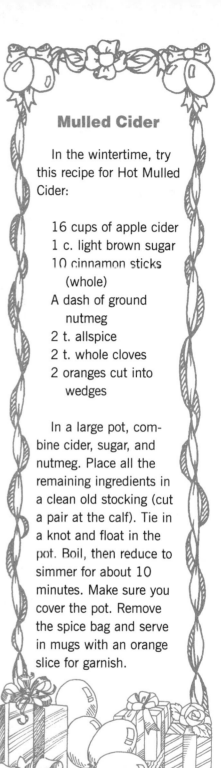

Mulled Cider

In the wintertime, try this recipe for Hot Mulled Cider:

- 16 cups of apple cider
- 1 c. light brown sugar
- 10 cinnamon sticks (whole)
- A dash of ground nutmeg
- 2 t. allspice
- 2 t. whole cloves
- 2 oranges cut into wedges

In a large pot, combine cider, sugar, and nutmeg. Place all the remaining ingredients in a clean old stocking (cut a pair at the calf). Tie in a knot and float in the pot. Boil, then reduce to simmer for about 10 minutes. Make sure you cover the pot. Remove the spice bag and serve in mugs with an orange slice for garnish.

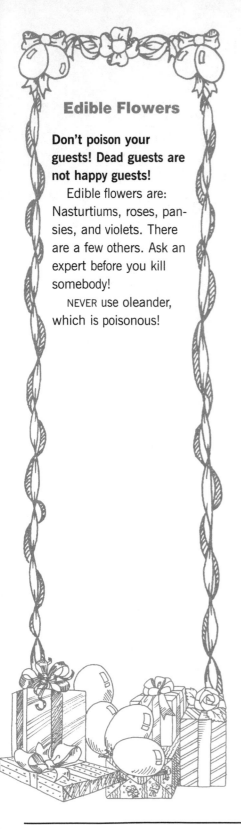

Edible Flowers

Don't poison your guests! Dead guests are not happy guests!

Edible flowers are: Nasturtiums, roses, pansies, and violets. There are a few others. Ask an expert before you kill somebody!

NEVER use oleander, which is poisonous!

Step 2: Look for a caterer with credentials! Meet four of them at least. Get someone certified by the state you live in as a real, true caterer. Find them through referral or recommendation. Call a few people they use as referrals and actually find out how they liked the service and the food! Taste their food samples.

Step 3: Get it in writing! Find out what the cancellation terms are; how much you have to deposit and when; how many people they will serve and for what price; what food exactly they will serve; if they will provide utensils, plates, etc. Know precisely what you are getting for what you are paying. Know what happens if they cancel or screw up, or if your mother-to-be breaks her engagement and you cancel the party. Lots of people have lost money on nonrefundable deposits this way.

Step 4: Do you like and trust the caterer? Have you met several of them? Do they make you feel pressured, like they are cramming things down your throat? Trust your instincts! Have you sampled their food? How many servers will show up at the event? You need at least two to run a banquet table, at least one bartender/drinks person, and two kitchen staff if you're having a buffet meal.

Step 5: Who is going to be in charge on the shower day? Will the person you are meeting actually show up? What will they do? What will be required of you, specifically? *Get everything in writing.*

Can I Cater Just Part of It?

Absolutely! There's no rule here! Your local deli would love to prepare some cold meat platters, hot dishes, or crudités! This is a great way to save time. Just make sure you confirm the contents of the platter and when you will pick it up. I suggest you pick it up yourself the morning of the shower, because sending someone else might mean the deli sends them home with vegetables when you were expecting a meat tray. The prices for these trays vary widely, but they sure help out in a pinch!

If you have the least bit of artistic flair, you can create great-looking trays much cheaper yourself. Buy some big disposable platters, some precut meats, some radishes and lettuce for garnishes. At $5.99 per pound for cold cuts, you'd still be ahead of the game, rolling and arranging each piece of meat yourself.

CHAPTER 8

Decorating Your Party

Decorating for the party is so much fun! Planning how you will decorate and make the environment interesting is exciting. You can create an ambience to match your theme using items appropriate to your theme, but there are some basics to decorating for every party: choosing the right colors, using flowers and the festive arrangement of food, using traditional decorations like paper goods and balloons.

It's easy to make all these things work together if you follow the simple ideas in this book. You're sure to have lots of ideas of your own to add. You can get everything to match, or you can make vibrant contrasts. Different colors stimulate people in different ways, so think about that when you are planning your shower. You may want to match the baby colors, or you may want to do something totally different. It's your choice!

Choosing Colors

Colors mean different things to different people. For my seven-year-old daughter and me, red and yellow always mean McDonald's, for instance. But did you know that the insides of prisons are often painted a pale rosy pink to calm the inmates? Did you know that lavender and pale blue are serene colors, while red and bright green stir things up? A cool, true indigo is thought to stimulate thinking, and purple is considered the most balanced color, representative of advanced spiritual enlightenment. Yellow is perceived as a happy color, and black as a sophisticated, chic statement, especially with metallic highlights. Gold means money, and silver supposedly means classy. What effect do you want to achieve at the shower?

Color Usage Lists

Just about the easiest way to stylize a party is to buy all the matching paper goods at once—before you even send out the invitations. Trot down to Michael's, Hallmark, or even Wal-Mart, and you'll find a whole section of matching paper goods. Or look under "Party" in your Yellow Pages, and you'll find these items, usually much cheaper, at party goods wholesale houses, especially if you live near a big city.

Items you can find that will match your chosen colors, theme, or the baby colors can include:

Invitations
Paper plates
Paper cups
Plastic flatware
Napkins
Streamers
Japanese lanterns
Glitter and sequins

Balloons
Piñatas
Signs
Posters
Banners
Swizzle sticks
Decorated toothpicks
Decorated straws
Curling ribbon
Fabric ribbon
Silk flowers
Crafter's spray paint
Place cards
Tablecloths
Precut veil (for making sachets or party favors)
Rolls of veil material
Scalloped veil material

Decorating the Shower Location

Decorating the shower is a really fun part of hosting it. In half an hour, all the fun items you've hoarded turn into a party atmosphere. How great! This section will give you general decorating ideas. If you have already chosen a specific theme, there are likely to be predictable decorations that go with it, or ones that are suggested in the theme description.

Decorating with Paper

There are many types of paper products you can get to decorate your party with. There are large accordion-fold baby things, streamers, piñatas, Chinese lanterns, luminarias, and many others. I cannot begin to tell you as much as you will learn from a trip to your party supply store. But I certainly can tell you a big secret about paper products: Unless you live in a very dry climate like Arizona in the summer, do not hang them out the day before! They will get limp and perhaps even be ruined, depending on your climate. I once strung streamers two days in advance of a party, thinking I was so organized to have it done early. The next morning, I woke up in my sunny Southern California home to find limp bits of paper hanging loosely around my living room! Disaster! I had to rush out and buy more. Lesson learned. Hang the party goods on the day of the party.

There are many ways to hang paper goods without destroying walls. If you have ceiling tiles, use bent-out large paper clips as holders for balloons and paper goods. If you have a regular flat ceiling, you can use flat thumbtacks—they work much better than push pins, which are often bright, call attention to themselves, and have a smaller head with which to affix the decoration. The tiny pinholes in your ceiling will hardly be noticeable. If you have a stucco ceiling, it is much better if you can avoid trying to nail anything directly into the ceiling, because you risk losing chunks of stucco. Instead, thumbtack your decorations to the opposite walls, or attach them to drapery rods with masking tape.

In the event that you really don't want to risk causing any sort of damage to the ceiling, buy some heavy-gauge fishing line at a sporting goods department. Make a knot in one end, poke the end of a thumbtack through the hole, and nail the tacks into the opposing walls, creating a sort of invisible spider's web on the ceiling. With minimal extra support required, it will hold up all your decorations and be easy to remove.

Decorating with Candles

Tapers that match your party colors, along with interesting candle-holders, are lovely. Put them in fishbowls, poke them into the cake, place an elegant silver candelabrum in the middle of your table, light a taper in the bathroom to light the way to that room. Candles are always appropriate for evening and night showers. Just be sure they won't tip accidentally and ignite a paper tablecloth, that no tipsy guest will burn himself reaching across them for food or drink, or that they will drip on food you want to serve.

Try decorating your candleholders with flowers, greenery, or even little plastic doo-dads, but don't use anything flammable, like paper. You might like to glue or tie tiny plastic figures from the party store to the candelabra or candleholders. Nice ideas might be a baby bottle or a pacifier tied up with ribbons and flowers.

You could also simply fill some pink, blue, and/or yellow baby bottles with sand and stick a candle in each of them. Make sure the candle won't melt the plastic of the bottle, but it should be fine if you fill the bottle to the top with sand and use a bobeche to prevent hot wax from pouring down. (It's always a good idea to use bobeches with candles, anyway, to prevent possible fire hazards and ruined tablecloths. A bobeche is a little glass ring that slips over the candle and forms a tray at its base to catch melted wax.)

Go back to Chapter 3, if you like, and read under "All-American Party" where I gave instructions on creating your very own pink, yellow, and blue candles. You can create any colors you want with the right crayons.

Decorating with Balloons

In the minds of most people, balloons mean it's a party! There are two different types of balloons—Mylar (the shiny metallic kind) and rubber (the only kind we had as kids). Mylar are often bigger, more expensive, and always filled with helium. Rubber can be filled with helium, water, or air.

Helium is typical for most parties. Make sure you don't fill the balloons with helium until the last couple of hours before the party, though, because it drains out in four or five hours and faster in full sunshine. Going to the florist's and ordering helium-filled balloons can be expensive, but that's one way to get them easily. Call a week in advance to order them for your big day. The other way to get them is to rent a helium tank from a party store. I even saw a small helium tank sold prefilled with some balloons at Target. Helium's combustible, so be careful driving it home, and keep the tank away from heat and flame. It took me about thirty minutes to fill up thirty balloons with the helium tank I bought for my daughter's birthday party. We tied brightly colored strings to them and put them all over the house, and sent each kid home with one or two. I also put them on the mailbox to signal that our house was the party place!

A very, very cool decorating trick is to create a "forest" of balloons on the ceiling, each trailing a long piece of curling ribbon. This would be especially cool if you have high ceilings. Or, you could do short ribbons and tie tiny plastic babies or baby gear to them. Make sure you tie several balloons to the special chair you'll create for the mother-to-be to sit in.

Decorating the Gift Table

The gift table is where you pile, stow, stack, and dump all the gifts that come for the shower. It is often decorated similarly to the buffet table. If you get fewer gifts than you predicted, simply put a plant or vase of flowers on the table at the last minute, before the mother-to-be shows up.

I suggest a "banquet table" about 6 feet in length for this purpose. You would have already picked out your table linens. If you are using a paper tablecloth and you find it does not cover the legs of your table and you want it to, take two plain white tablecloths (paper, plastic, cotton, damask) and slide one down over the front so it covers the legs of the table and touches the floor. Tape it down wherever it comes to on the table with heavy duct tape (the wide silver kind of tape). Cover the tape and whatever overlap with the other white tablecloth.

Do you want to keep your paper-products theme—the pattern on the paper goods you bought for the party? Try the following suggestions.

If you are using a cloth tablecloth underneath: Fold the matching paper tablecloth in half, pretty side out, down the center. Ruck or crinkle or gather it in a nice way. With a ruler, determine the exact middle of your buffet table. Pin it to the table with a large safety pin, using the inside of the pin as a sort of ring. Complete the same on both ends of the table. If you want lovely hanging trails, or if it doesn't reach, add some matching ribbon and pin that to it, too. Don't worry about the pins being ugly. You can wire flowers or bows to them to cover them up.

If you are using a paper tablecloth underneath: Read the instructions above. However, instead of using pins (which would rip your tablecloth), use bits of wire to hold up the decorative paper cloth or ribbons that you poke through the paper tablecloth and tape securely to the flat surface of the table underneath.

The same method works with ribbons or real or fake flower garlands, like maybe fake English Ivy or matching roses. (Look for 6–8-foot-long garlands of silk flowers at the local crafts or floral supply store.)

This material is repeated in the "Buffet Table" section, but I figured if you weren't serving a meal, you might not see it there and then would not have the information you need.

When You're Ready to Think about Seating Arrangements . . .

If you have decided to have a buffet, everyone pretty much expects to fill their plates and find their own place to sit. The only time you really need to worry about everyone sitting at a table is at a barbecue, a formal meal, or when the mother-to-be is opening the presents.

Here's how to plan the seating: If you have the shower out-doors, you can rent nifty garden furniture; take any sturdy metal-legged stuff out of your house and put it in the yard, and let people sit on benches, lawn chairs, or whatever. If you are doing it on the grass, DON'T take out any wooden-legged furniture, and test the ground first to make sure it's hard enough to hold someone sit-ting on it. Some little chair legs will sink right into the dirt and topple your guest!

You can make benches from two really large planters (with something in them, like a big plant!) and two 2" × 4" pieces of lumber. You can rent lawn chairs or make this the perfect occasion to justify buying that patio furniture you have your eye on.

If you are doing it inside, you can also bring in lawn chairs, especially if they aren't too ratty-looking. Usually, the mother-to-be sits in the best chair in the house, and it's decorated specially for her. Everyone else is arranged in a sort of horseshoe shape, espe-cially for gift opening. Set up seating so people can sit in groups of two or more, preferably with little tables to put their stuff on nearby.

Many rental companies have chairs (and tables, too) they'd love to rent to you fairly cheaply. In most cases, they will come set them up and take them down the next day for no extra charge. Compare this with the cost of buying basic resin chairs at the home supply store before you rent them, though. You may find that if you plan to throw more than two parties this year and you can afford the storage space, it's better to buy than rent.

I bought some wonderful padded metal folding chairs at a big discount warehouse for about $25 each. My local rental company will rent something similar to me for $8.50 per chair. That means in three uses, I've paid for the chairs. And if I decide I don't want to store them, I can always sell them.

Another way to get adequate seating is to ask guests who have folding lawn furniture to loan it to you. Pick it up or have them drop it off the day before the party, though, so people aren't moving furniture at the very last moment.

Creating the Seat of Honor

Your mother-to-be is the guest of honor at your shower, even if the mayor's there. She should have a special chair with optimal views of all the other guests, especially during the gift-opening part of the shower.

One of your wingback chairs will work just fine, as would a captain's chair from your dining room. Decorate it in advance with balloons and lay a streamer across the seat that says "Reserved for Betsy." You could drape it in velvet, plump it up with extra cushions, or spray paint an old chair gold and glue fake jewels from the hobby store to it. You could tie baby things to its back; spray paint it swirls of pink, yellow and blue, and if you have experienced mothers in the group and this isn't her first, you could add a comedic touch by putting a plastic washbasin below with a sign that says, "Just in case your water breaks during the shower."

If You're Doing It at Home . . .

A word of caution: If you have fabric-covered sofas, you might want to consider buying a can of Scotchgard and spraying your sofas or chairs a day or two before the event. Nobody is going to want to spill anything, but a lot of people in a small space getting all excited sometimes causes boo-boos. And a big red-wine boo-boo on your white sofa is probably one shower souvenir you don't want!

You may have to rethink your furniture layout for the evening. Your lovely curio etagere is at risk if your room is crowded. Why not slip it into your bedroom for the party? And as for all those extraneous things we keep in living rooms that take up space, why not get rid of those, too, if you'll already be squeezed in. Nobody's going to be thinking about how stark your decorating style is if you shuffle everything off to your bedroom to make room for fifteen folding chairs and a sofa.

HELP! I Need Furniture!

Whatever you can think of for this party, somebody somewhere has it for rent, or to buy, cheap. There are hundreds of things you can rent that will help you deal with your decorating. They are usually reasonably priced, and you might be able to get the rental company to set them up and take them down for a minimal charge.

Let me tell you this story, though, before you rush out to rent anything you need for the party: I once was planning to have sixty people from my husband's office over for dinner at the same time. I needed two banquet tables for the event. I called the rental company, and they wanted $15 each for the tables, which seemed reasonable at the time. I threw big parties about six times a year, and renting the tables at $15 each ($30 per time), six times per year, would have cost me $180 a year.

Luckily, I went into a hardware store (who would have thought?) and saw the same tables on sale. They were really the identical tables. They were $30 each! I also use them for craft projects and for Thanksgiving and other events. Total investment = $60. So before you rush out to rent something, you might want to check out if it is less expensive to buy it.

The rule of thumb is this: If you will use it more than three times in your life, it's probably cheaper to buy it than rent it. The same is true for lawn furniture. If you have been planning to buy some someday anyway, why not use this as the perfect excuse? Thinking about this makes owning a rental company look like a pretty amazing business, doesn't it?

Tableware

As you see in the rental box in this section, you can rent nice stuff from any company. From plates to glasses to serving dishes, the local rental company doubtless has it all. But if you are like me and want to throw it all away and be done with it, I suggest you buy paper or plastic tableware, including napkins, tablecloths, plates, cups, and silverware. My motto is, Why wash it when you can toss it?

All about Party Flowers

Flowers are one of the more fun parts of a shower. You'll want a nice centerpiece for the table, a tiny bouquet for the bathroom, and maybe a nice flat arrangement for your coffee table, if you're doing this at home.

The most obvious choice is to pay somebody to make these bouquets for you. But if you don't want to spend an extra $50 on flowers, take these tips I learned from Tess Kenna at Winslow Floral in Winslow, Arizona. You just might find you have a real knack for it!

First, decide what colors you want. If your party colors match the baby colors, you can probably figure out flowers that match all by your lonesome. Or stroll through a couple of flower shops. Some better grocery stores sell blooms "by the stem," which is how loose flowers are purchased.

Pick out the kind of flowers you want a few days before the party, but don't buy them until the last minute (that day). You can buy them in the morning for an evening shower if (a) it's cold in your house, (b) you have room in your fridge to store the bouquets/arrangements, or (c) you have no other choice.

Look for flowers without browning edges, and roses that are firm when you squeeze them. Check the base of the flower for tears: this is how florists make roses look younger than they are—they tear off the dying petals from around the outside. You can tell if you look closely. Get the freshest flowers you can. Buy with them a bunch of "leather," those wonderful glossy fern fronds you see in flower arrangements, and some baby's breath (gypsophila) unless you have great, hardy yard flowers at home.

From the florist, ask for a brick of Oasis, which is the green stuff they poke flowers into. (You can also get this at a crafts store.) The florist will probably charge you a buck or so. Ask also for a piece of florist's wire (long, skinny green-coated wire, any size will do fine). If the flowers don't come with a longevity agent, ask for some. This is the powder you mix with the water to make the flowers last longer.

When you get home, fill buckets with water and add the longevity agent. Immediately cut the stems and at once, without

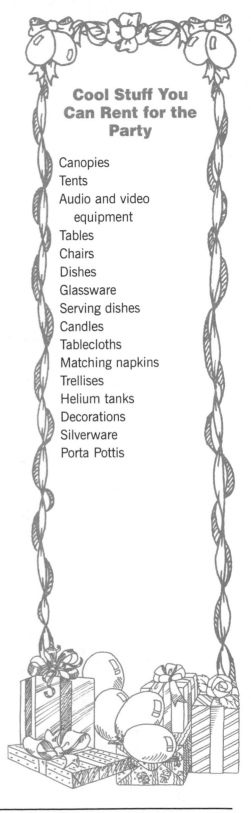

Cool Stuff You Can Rent for the Party

Canopies
Tents
Audio and video
   equipment
Tables
Chairs
Dishes
Glassware
Serving dishes
Candles
Tablecloths
Matching napkins
Trellises
Helium tanks
Decorations
Silverware
Porta Pottis

seconds passing, put the flowers into the water. Every second costs the flowers life. Florists cut the stems one at a time and plunk them into the water instantly.

Put the Oasis into a bucket or sink full of water to which you have added the longevity agent. Oasis floats, so weight it with a pot or something. It will fill with water in a while. Give it thirty minutes to soak.

Next, select a pretty, low dish or flowerpot or two. Get a sharp knife, your cutting board, and some veined packing tape, duct tape, or florist's tape. Take your wire and use it to cut the Oasis to fit into your pots or dishes. (Cut it like you see them cutting people's necks with wire in gory guy movies.) Stuff little bits of Oasis into the pockets around the sides so it is totally full of green matter—nowhere is there air between the pot and the Oasis. Now tape the Oasis into the pots or dishes with your tape. Two strips in each direction for a pot 6 inches or more in diameter is plenty.

Repeat three times, "This is fun, this is fun."

Take the leather fern and "green the bowl." That means, poke the fronds into the dish or pot so that they leave little spaces, or whorls, where a bloom would fit perfectly, foiled by the dark fern. You will use all the bunch of leather fern on two 6-inch flowerpots. Snip the ends of the fern so the part where the leaf begins is the part resting on the Oasis.

Now, go run around your yard with a pair of pruning shears, picking any wee leafy branches (young lemon or orange branches are lovely) or other interesting plants or flowers you see. Try to avoid garden flowers—except hardy roses, marigolds, hollyhocks, delphiniums, and purple statice—because they will wilt quickly. Stick them at once into a pitcher of water.

Now get your refrigerated flowers out of the fridge. Quickly cut their bases with the paring knife and immediately poke them into the whorls you created with the leather. (The longer you leave a flower's stem exposed to air, the less time it will live. Imagine an air bubble in a diver's bloodstream, and you get the idea. Florists try to cut it to seconds between snipping the stem and arranging the flower.) Add your yard plants.

Fuss a little if you must, but remember, flower arranging is like geometry—everything in balance. You cannot put six white roses left of center and three right—it will look funny. A simple idea is imagining the bowl cut in half. Put half your blooms on either side, far enough apart so you can enjoy looking at all their petals. Add some filler (either gypsophila from the florist or your yard plants) and you're nearly done.

If you have to pull out the flowers a few times, that's normal. Even professional designers modify their works of art. Mess around with it, have fun, and in a few minutes, voilà! You will have a worthy and attractive centerpiece and a wonderful table spray. Take a few of the extra blooms, slip them into a vase (with treated water in it), and put it in your bathroom.

If you want, tie a balloon or two to small sticks and poke them into the bouquet, too. Stuff in a bow or two, or something else interesting. Maybe wire some of the leftover favor supplies (like plastic babies and tiny storks) to long skewers and poke them in, too.

Congratulations! You're a florist! And you just saved at least $50.

Decorating Your Buffet Table

First, never crowd zillions of foods onto a tray. Ideally, they should not even touch the sides of the tray or platter. Get more platters, or make them from florists' colored foil wrapped around sheets of wood or heavy cardboard. Have backup trays and refresh them by exchanging them when they get more than two-thirds emptied.

Select a specific table for the food and a separate one for drinks if you're expecting to serve more than one or two beverage choices. I suggest a banquet table about 6 feet in length for the purposes of the meal you would serve to fifteen women. You can probably rent one for $15, or buy one for $30 at the hardware store or Office Depot or Home Depot. They store flat, so if you like to entertain, buy it, don't rent it.

You will have already picked out your table linens, so let's say this here: If you find your paper tablecloth does not cover the legs of your table and you want it to, take two plain white tablecloths

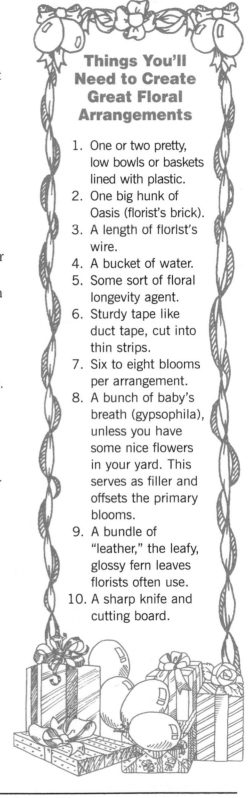

Things You'll Need to Create Great Floral Arrangements

1. One or two pretty, low bowls or baskets lined with plastic.
2. One big hunk of Oasis (florist's brick).
3. A length of florist's wire.
4. A bucket of water.
5. Some sort of floral longevity agent.
6. Sturdy tape like duct tape, cut into thin strips.
7. Six to eight blooms per arrangement.
8. A bunch of baby's breath (gypsophila), unless you have some nice flowers in your yard. This serves as filler and offsets the primary blooms.
9. A bundle of "leather," the leafy, glossy fern leaves florists often use.
10. A sharp knife and cutting board.

(paper, plastic, cotton, damask) and slide one down over the front so it covers the legs of the table and touches the floor. Tape it down wherever it comes to on the table, with heavy duct tape (the wide silver kind of tape). Cover the tape and whatever overlap with the other white tablecloth.

Do you want to keep your paper products theme—the pattern on the paper goods you bought for the party? Try the following suggestions.

If you are using a cloth tablecloth underneath: Fold the matching paper tablecloth in half, pretty side out, down the center. Ruck or crinkle or gather it in a nice way. With a ruler, determine the exact middle of your buffet table. Pin it to the table with a large safety pin. Complete the same on both ends of the table. If you want lovely hanging trails, or if it doesn't reach, add some matching ribbon and pin that to it, too. Don't worry about the pins being ugly. You can wire flowers or bows to them to cover them up.

If you are using a paper tablecloth underneath: Read the preceding instructions. However, instead of using pins (which would rip your tablecloth), use bits of wire to hold up the decorative paper cloth or ribbons that you poke through the paper tablecloth and tape securely to the flat surface of the table underneath.

The same method works with ribbons or real or fake flower garlands, like maybe fake English Ivy or matching roses. (Look for 6–8-foot-long garlands of silk flowers at the local crafts or floral supply store.)

Decorating the Tabletop

Stack three or four large books, like encyclopedias or dictionaries, slightly off of center on your table. Cover the entire stack with a matching paper tablecloth or a wonderful piece of fabric (velvet? brocade? something that matches the theme of your party?). You can either wrap it around the bottom of the stack, or you can let it flow onto the table surface.

On top of this, you can put the floral bouquet you made, the shower cake, some interesting centerpiece tied to your theme, whatever. If you put out a simple vase of flowers, make it a nice vase and put something a wee bit lower under the vase for variety's sake. (Like a small silver box, a wee plastic baby doll, a small ceramic bird, etc.)

If you want to put your buffet on different levels, make the stack with the centerpiece highest, and place another dish, maybe a salad in a lovely bowl, on the next tier down.

You may want to run garlands from the centerpiece down to one or more corners of the table. Or you can artfully sprinkle some flower petals or leaves (at the last minute), glitter, brightly colored diaper pins, or sequins around the table.

Planning Table Layout

Try out where your platters will go on the table, including where you will stack the plates and how you will arrange the silverware, napkins, and any garnishes or other decorations on the table now. Remember, your goal is to move people through the line, not give them reason to dawdle, because people behind them will be waiting. Put the plates, napkins, and silverware at one side, near one another. This is where the line forms. Make sure there is room for people to line up here. Plan to put your pastas and salads next, followed by your main courses. If you are not serving a meal, put the cake in the center, precut, with the snacks and crudités all around it, but with the plates and napkins still to one side.

Think movement. If the room necessitates that the guests enter on the left and flow right across the table, set it up that way. If you are using a round table, plan a circular flow. Physically walk around the table, holding a plate. Does it feel right the way you've planned it? Move it the other way. Will fifteen women end up clumped against the wall of your dining room? Will they have to jump out the window to get back to the living room? The most common mistake is stacking plates and/or napkins at opposite ends of the buffet table. Don't do this. Put all that stuff together. Otherwise, people will be confused and will screw up your line and it won't move smoothly.

Now is the time to figure out which utensils you will use. You will destroy your careful decor if you have to put a black plastic serving spoon on your pink chiffon tablecloth. Figure now to buy

or rent appropriate utensils for everything you'll be serving. Most discount gift stores sell cheap silver-plated serving utensils that will look nice for the party. If you want to dress up plain old everyday ones, tie matching ribbons to them and hot glue small silk flowers to the centers of the bows. Cut streamers short so they don't get in the food.

Your table arrangement should lead to appealing views of the food from each angle, as well as facilitate efficient movement through the line. You will begin with plates, then salads, then breads or pastas, and then the main course at the end. This will make it all move much more smoothly AND prevent people from taking more than they can eat, we predict.

Garnishing Your Platters

Now's as good a time as any to think about how you will garnish these platters. You can do it with flowers, interesting toothpicks, little plastic doo-dads you bought at the party store, interesting lettuces (radicchio, romaine, Bibb), or real outside greenery, or you can make the garnishes. There are dozens of books on garnishes, so I am going to give you directions for the two I use for baby showers. These are so easy you'll be embarrassed by all the compliments you'll get.

Making Apple Birds

What you'll need:
Two large, unblemished red apples
Two whole cloves
Several bamboo skewers
2 T. of lemon juice and a cotton ball
A paring knife
Half a potato or the second apple
Some greenery, like leaves or lettuce or parsley

How to do it:
Read these directions through before you begin cutting!

1. With a paring knife, cut just a little less than ¼ of the apple out of the whole. (Leave the remainder intact.) Don't cut all the way down to the core. This piece will become the bird's neck and head. The part directly opposite the slice-away is now the bird's body. The bottom of the apple is his little tush. Twist off the stem. This is where the head will be attached.

2. Put a little water into a bowl with the lemon juice, and put the piece you've just cut into it. Swab out the exposed section with the diluted lemon juice.

3. Leaving a gap of about ¼ inch from the exposed section, cut out the wing section by cutting a wedge from the bird's side. Don't cut all the way to the core. Repeat for other side. You will now have two thin flaps forming a V on the top of the bird.

4. Swab cuts with lemon juice, and dip the wedges into the lemon juice.

5. Take one wedge and gently slice a slightly smaller section out, creating a tiny canoe shape with even thickness. Repeat slightly smaller, then slightly smaller until only the tiniest piece of the wedge is left, barely more than the skin. You should have three or maybe four tiny apple canoes. Repeat for other side. These will become the feathers.

6. Dip them all into the lemon-juice mixture.

7. Slice the potato or other apple in half. You are now creating a stand for your bird.

8. Poke two lengths of the bamboo skewers (about 2 inches) into the bird's body where you'd expect the legs to be. Poke the other end into the base. Check that he stands all by himself without falling over. If he does, move the skewers until he balances himself sturdily.

9. Remove the largest piece of the apple canoe or wedge from the lemon juice and put it into the crevice on the wing side of the bird, slightly off from the front. Repeat with next smallest

piece and so on. Repeat on other side. If the wings keep sliding off, either blot them with a paper towel or skewer them with a toothpick. Cap the toothpick with the tiniest scrap of skin from the last cut.

10. The color contrast between the white and red makes it look like feathers. The wing will extend well behind the bird's tush.

11. For the head, take the first section you cut out of the bird. Cut a V-shape that roughly matches the depth of the V you cut in the apple by the stem when you cut this piece out. This is where you will attach the head.

12. Cut a thin neck and a head rather arrowhead shaped, coming to a point, at the opposite end. Dip in lemon juice. Attach to the neck (where the stem of the apple was) with one or two pieces of broken bamboo skewer. Trim his neck if it looks too thick.

13. Press in each whole clove to make the eyes.

14. To make a fancy tail, take the other half of an apple and cut it into a V that roughly matches the size of the V you cut out for the very first slice in step 1.

15. Repeat step 9 to make a grand feathered tail. Affix the tail with two pieces of vertical bamboo skewer. Remember to dip each slice in the lemon-juice mix. Fan the pieces out and attach them with a piece or two of skewer stuck horizontally into the bird's bottom.

16. Put him where you want him—like the middle of a cheese-and-cracker platter, and garnish his base with the greenery you selected. Sound hard? It takes only about fifteen minutes the first time and has an amazing dramatic presentation.

Making a Watermelon Baby Carriage

What you'll need:

A seedless watermelon, whole, with a lovely overall color. Find one where the yellowish spot is on the bottom and when you put it on a flat surface, it doesn't roll or sit lopsided.

A sharp paring knife with a very firm blade

A large serving platter

Some sort of garnish (lettuce, parsley, something similar)

A melon baller

A ruler

A toothpick

About a 6-inch piece of yellow ribbon

An orange

Two wooden skewers; one broken into four pieces, one broken in half

Fruit salad ingredients (cut-up apples, bananas, pineapple chunks, shredded coconut, mandarin orange sections, mango chunks, etc.)

A long carving knife or electric knife

How to do it:

Read the directions completely before you begin!

1. Wash the watermelon. Put the flattest side of the watermelon down on the counter. The "length" of the watermelon is now considered from stem to stern. The "width" is the distance between the side lying on the counter and your smiling face looking down at the watermelon. In other words, the vertical distance of the melon.

2. With the carving knife, make a vertical cut right down the middle of the width of the watermelon until you have cut straight down about one-third of its entire width.

3. Now cut the watermelon lengthwise from the stem side all the way until it connects with your vertical cut. Remove the section and save it so you can add watermelon balls to your fruit salad.

4. The part that arches up is now the "hood" of the baby carriage, and the bulky base of the melon is the carriage part.

5. Take the section you cut off and cut out its center like this: Cut a rectangle, leaving about 1-inch of the removed piece intact. Discard the rectangle. The remaining piece becomes the handle of the carriage. Affix it to the carriage using the wooden skewer cut in half.

6. Ball out all the melon inside and put it into a large bowl. With the paring knife, cut the pink part off the inside of the hood. If you'd like to get fancy, scallop the edge. Scrape out

any excess with a teaspoon. Place on garnished serving platter.

7. Slice the orange in four thick slices. Affix each "wheel" to the base of the melon using the wooden skewer broken into four pieces.

8. You now have an empty "basket" to hold your fruit salad. To make it prettier, follow the rest of the steps. Take your paring knife and cut little scallops out all the way around the edge of the lip of the carriage (the horizontal cuts on the watermelon). Continue up and over the handle.

9. Take the yellow ribbon (or pink or blue if you know the baby's gender) and make a bow. Affix it to the center of the hood with the toothpick thrust deeply into the white part of the hood.

10. Using your paring knife, mark a lattice pattern on the handle of the basket. Cut out the little diamond shapes all over the handle with your paring knife. Support the back of the handle (obviously taking care not to cut yourself) when you make your slices. Or invent your own pattern.

11. Use a toothpick to attach more bows, some flowers, or anything else to the top of the handle, or tie ribbons around the sides.

12. You're done! Add fruit salad ingredients to the balled melon, fill the basket, and voila! An impressive fruit salad bowl with minimum effort. However DO NOT lift the basket by the handle! Garnish the platter you will set it on any way you desire, but flowers are particularly nice.

Choosing the Right Music

Music is such a personal thing! Some people are heavily influenced by the sounds around them, and for them playing sad or melancholy at your party would be a real downer. Further, some folks don't like rock and roll (hard to imagine, isn't it?), and some very intense people might be offended by Led Zeppelin lyrics. Unless you've chosen a shower that has a musical theme, for example, Elvis Commemorative or "Nifty '50s Party," you're going to have to think a bit about what you want to play.

First, do you and your mother-to-be want the music to be mellow and refined? Classical would be nice, but it's often interruptive at a party to have cymbals clashing. If you are going classical, which is an excellent choice for most parties, may I suggest you pick up a Baroque medley CD? Did you know that Baroque music actually stimulates the cerebral cortex of the brain and generates fresh ideas? (This was allegedly tested on a number of employees in big corporations.)

If serenity is the key to your party—try Enya's *Shepherd Moon*, a Gregorian chant, Vivaldi's *Four Seasons*, Celine Dion's *C'est Deux*, anything from Wyndham Hill, Narada, Wynton Marsalis, or James Galway. There are quite a few nice Celtic CDs available right now; many make nice background music. Looking for something more rowdy? Pick your favorites and ask the mother-to-be for hers. Or try the tried-n-true party favorites for thirty-somethings—Rod Stewart, Billy Joel, Bruce Springsteen, The Eagles, and so on.

Right now there are a lot of "golden oldies" and "dance classics" CDs around that you can pick up for under $10 usually. I'm not happy to admit that some of my favorite songs are now available in montage. (I once read that the definition of growing older is "Your favorite music is now available through television ads for two easy payments on your credit card"—It's a scary thing!)

You should have, borrow, or rent a nice stereo system for the party. Set the speakers in opposite corners in the main room for the party, and test them in advance.

CHAPTER 9

Women Bearing Gifts

Does the Hostess Traditionally Get the Mother-to-be a Gift?

It is customary for the hostess to get the mother-to-be a gift for the shower, just like everyone else. You might want to coordinate the buying of a major gift, or you might want to give her something small but very nice just from you if the shower is really setting you back financially.

We All Want to Buy Her a Big Gift. How Do I Handle That?

Does your mother-to-be need a crib? A baby swing? A stroller? A new washing machine so she can do all those diapers? Getting a big gift is exciting! You can easily keep this part of the shower a secret from the mother-to-be even if the shower isn't.

Here's how to get money from people—tell them you want to buy Rita a crib. If they know it's a big item, they're liable to put up more than the $20 they were planning on spending on a shower gift. When they hand you the money, hand them the card to sign.

What if you get through all your guests and you're still lower on cash than you can personally make up comfortably? Try calling one or two of the big donors again, or call the grandparents-to-be. If you get through all the guests and you have more money than it will cost, buy relevant objects: crib sheets and blankets, stuffed animals, etc. Make sure everyone who sends money has his or her name on the card, even if you have to write it on yourself.

Presenting the Big Gift

You could have some handsome, burly college guys deliver it during the shower. You could have some guys set it in the front yard after she's safely inside obliviously enjoying the shower, then take her outside with all the guests to surprise her. You could have it in your living room when she gets there, with a big red bow on it. You could drape a cloth over it, stick some flowers on it, hide it in a corner of your room and ta-daa! Unveil it during the gift portion of your shower.

When Does She Open Gifts?

She can open them either before or after the food is served but probably not during. Think about the time of your shower—will the guests be ravenous when they get there? If it is potluck, will the food cool down too much while you wait? I suggest she opens the gifts AFTER the meal but before the cake.

What's the Best Way to Record What She Gets from Whom?

Make a copy of your guest list. Next to each guest's name, have a line on which you can have someone, preferably not you, write down who gave what. Another way is to collect the cards attached to the gifts and write the object given on the back of each. Or you could simply have a sheet of paper and a pen for the guest who sits right next to the mother-to-be to list who gave what. Know this: Your mother-to-be will NOT remember and neither will you, so don't rely on her.

Does She Need to Write Thank-You Notes for Everything?

Writing thank-you notes is never wrong, but it's really only necessary if someone sends a gift to the shower but cannot attend herself. As hostess, you would be the one who knows this. If the mother-to-be personally and warmly thanks each friend as the gift is opened, she need do no more. If you know she's going to want to handwrite

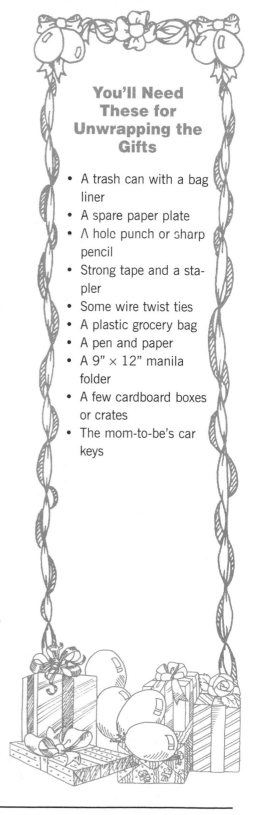

You'll Need These for Unwrapping the Gifts

- A trash can with a bag liner
- A spare paper plate
- A hole punch or sharp pencil
- Strong tape and a stapler
- Some wire twist ties
- A plastic grocery bag
- A pen and paper
- A 9" × 12" manila folder
- A few cardboard boxes or crates
- The mom-to-be's car keys

them anyway, get a pen and note pad and assign someone at the shower who knows most of the guests the task of writing down who gave what along with a brief description of the item.

After She's Unwrapped Everything

Put the list of who gave what and all the cards into the manila folder. Now, all the wrapping paper is neatly stored in the trash can with the liner bag, so it will be easy for you to get rid of it.

Put all the gifts and the manila envelope into the crates so she can take them home, and have someone help put them in her trunk.

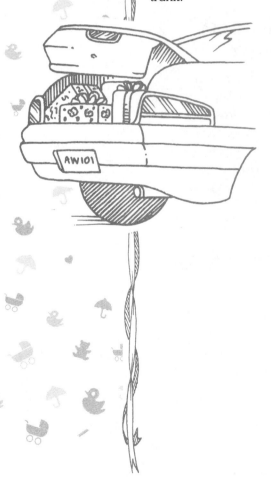

CHAPTER 10

Seamless Party Management 101

This chapter is about how to manage the people who are helping you set up the party, how to manage the guests, and how to make a backup plan in case someone falls through.

The Taming of the Shrew

First, although, of course, you always are, be polite to everyone who is helping you, whether they are being paid or not. As the tensions mount, and particularly if this is the first event you've handled, you might become a shrew. I used to become a shrew in the few hours before an event. I would just go nuts when someone called at the last minute to say they couldn't do or bring or that I had never ordered something, et cetera. So chill out, sister! Plan for a little bit of insanity, a touch of imperfection, and trust your own organizational skills. That's secret number one. Chill out.

Let Your Fingers Do the Talking

The second secret of good staff management is phone numbers. Yep, that's it. For everybody who says they are going to do something, write down what it is they are promising to do or bring, what their numbers are, and when they will call you to confirm that they are doing or bringing it. Call them the week before to remind them what they promised. Expect surprises. That's why you, the consummate shower thrower, have secret number three . . .

Have a Backup Plan for Your Backup Plan

While this obviously isn't brain surgery, people are the unpredictable factor in all your planning, and things will go wrong. Those of you who share my perfectionist tendencies will want to maim whoever thwarts the perfect shower you have planned, but we will avert disaster with a great backup plan.

Here's how it works:

1. If you are doing it potluck, have two of everything coming (e.g., two green salads, two casseroles, two fruit salads, etc.).

2. No matter how you are preparing the food, know that for the right price, at the last minute you can get the local deli, grocery store, or convenience package to smooth over the rough spots. No green salads? Go get the prepackaged, pre-washed lettuce for $2.39 and a premade Caesar salad kit. One minute later, you've got the missing salad on the table.

3. The bakery screwed up the cake and it says "Happy Sixth Birthday, Tommy!" which you noticed after you got it home. Fine. Lose Tommy's name with a cold knife on a chilled cake. (The icing will lift right off.) Replace it with your own message, using a tube of decorator's gel (from the baking goods section). Tommy's cake is decorated like a dinosaur? Sprinkle it with some colorful flakes and a plastic whatever you bought to decorate the table with, and add some non-poisonous flowers.

See? Everything is remediable. Worse things would include rain on your garden party. You would have called in advance, however, to make sure you had a backup location or a party-rental place ready to bring you a big waterproof canopy on a half-hour's notice. It might cost a bit more, but at least it won't ruin your party!

The bottom line of backup plans is: Try not to need one. Call the people you are counting on, even the professionals (bakers, caterers, musicians), to confirm a week ahead, and if you know someone is a space cadet, call also the day before. You are entitled to be nutty. In the words of the whining song from the '60s, or a very close rendition thereof: "It's my party and I'll panic if I want to, panic if I want to, panic if I want to . . ." Choose not to panic by following the steps in this book for a flawless event.

One of My Cohosts Keeps Screwing Up. Now What Do I Do?

Is she:

(a) Promising to do something and then not finding the time/money to do it?

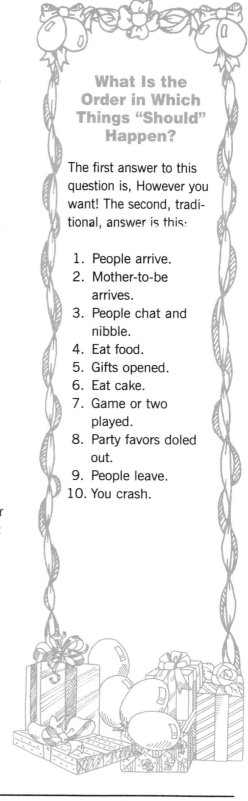

(b) Doing something wrong? (Like overspending on the budget consistently?)

(c) Doing too much and getting in everyone's way?

(d) Bickering with the other cohosts/helpers?

(e) Agreeing to do something one way and then doing it differently anyway?

(f) Other annoying things that make you wish you could dump her?

Solving Problem (a) "Promising to Do Something and Then Not Finding the Time/Money to Do It"

If she agreed on the delegation chart at your first meeting to take on responsibilities and now she is not following through, it could be because of lack of time, lack of interest, or lack of money. You're the boss, so you get to find out what it is. In a non-confrontational manner, give her a call or meet her for coffee. After a little small talk, say precisely this:

Debbie, I really appreciate that you want to help out with Pam's baby shower. When we had our first meeting, you took some responsibilities that you seemed to really want to do. But we're getting closer to the shower and I don't see these things getting done. I'm wondering how I can help you so they do get done. What's going on for you?

If she complains that she will do it, she just hasn't had time, and you're running out of time, tell her you understand but that you would like this done. Either give her a short deadline (like, you have to have it by Tuesday) or tell her you'd really like to let Sarah help out, too, with the party. Would it be OK with her if you let Sarah do this one task since Debbie is so busy?

If you suspect that the answer is that she doesn't have the money, you might want to say that you found an extra few bucks in the budget. Would it be OK if you gave her the money so she could finish her assignments?

If you think that for some reason she's just simply lost interest, the kindest way to end it is to end it. "Debbie, I really appreciate all you've done so far for Pam's shower. I know you really want to help, but I see that things aren't getting done. It seems to me like you have so much going on in your life right now you just don't have time for this stuff. Let me assign your tasks to Belinda, and you just show up at the shower, OK?"

Solving Problem (b) "Doing Something Wrong"

Some people simply don't follow directions, no matter what they agree to do. If you knew this person in advance was like this, you really have no one to blame but yourself. But if this is a surprise to you about your cohost, there are ways to fix it depending on your patience level.

If she's overspending, you could say, "Ramona, we agreed to a budget. You have a copy of the budget. We agreed that if you overspent, it would come out of your own money. I cannot pay the difference between what we budgeted and what you spent on cloth napkins when we agreed on paper, even though they are prettier. You're going to have to make up the difference yourself or take them back."

If she's buying the wrong colors, losing things, or basically being an airhead, and you are a saint (I never am in these situations), you could say, "Tiffany, I need to go to the party goods store, too. Why don't we go together on Saturday?"

If you are not a saint and she's an airhead, you could do what I have done. "Stephanie, I know you want to help with Linda's shower, and I appreciate that. But the last five things you were supposed to do haven't turned out like we'd planned. I think maybe you ought to let me/someone else handle the rest of this and you just show up at the shower as one of the cohosts. I don't want to overburden you with things to do when you have other things on your mind."

Solving Problem (c) "Doing Too Much and Getting in Everyone's Way"

Ah, you have an overzealous aide-de-camp! How charming! This person's natural energy to make things just right can work in your favor if you refocus their energy.

Although it may come from "I-can-do-this-better-than-she-can" thinking, the people who act this way are usually starved for attention and responsibility. Although it sounds totally infantile, giving it to them will probably solve your problem. As the party planner, you are the authority figure.

If the zealot is one of your cohosts, you're in great luck. All you need to do is take her to lunch. Tell her what an incredible job you think she is doing with her segment of the party, and give her more responsibilities, since she's "proven she's so capable." Tell her something like, "Lisa, you've been great! Thanks so much for all the energy you've been putting into Sylvia's shower. My gosh, what would we do without you? I'm wondering if it would be too much to ask you to take on a little more responsibility?"

Of course, she'll say yes. Then assign her something like making all the party favors, setting up the gift table, or something else that is an overload task for another division. When she agrees to do it, tell her how relieved you feel.

If necessary, mention that you and she know how capable she is, but that this party is a real opportunity for Gretchen, the other cohost, to really give something creative to Sylvia. Could she please leave Gretchen to do her work as she sees fit?

Most people will take this and run with it. I doubt you'll have much more meddling. But if you do, be stronger in your suggestions. Mostly, meddlesome people simply are looking for extreme acknowledgment for their small contributions.

Solving Problem (d) "Bickering with the Other Cohosts/Helpers"

Bickering is such a silly waste of time, and yet sometimes groups of women get competitive and do it. It's really quite silly when you think about it, but as the party planner, you get to

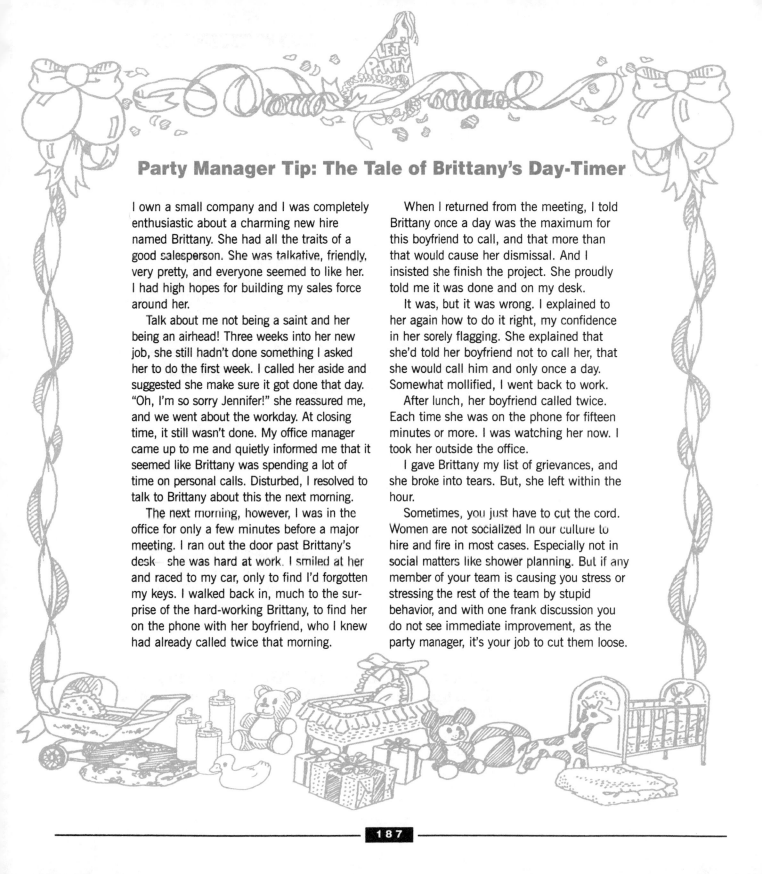

Party Manager Tip: The Tale of Brittany's Day-Timer

I own a small company and I was completely enthusiastic about a charming new hire named Brittany. She had all the traits of a good salesperson. She was talkative, friendly, very pretty, and everyone seemed to like her. I had high hopes for building my sales force around her.

Talk about me not being a saint and her being an airhead! Three weeks into her new job, she still hadn't done something I asked her to do the first week. I called her aside and suggested she make sure it got done that day. "Oh, I'm so sorry Jennifer!" she reassured me, and we went about the workday. At closing time, it still wasn't done. My office manager came up to me and quietly informed me that it seemed like Brittany was spending a lot of time on personal calls. Disturbed, I resolved to talk to Brittany about this the next morning.

The next morning, however, I was in the office for only a few minutes before a major meeting. I ran out the door past Brittany's desk—she was hard at work. I smiled at her and raced to my car, only to find I'd forgotten my keys. I walked back in, much to the surprise of the hard-working Brittany, to find her on the phone with her boyfriend, who I knew had already called twice that morning.

When I returned from the meeting, I told Brittany once a day was the maximum for this boyfriend to call, and that more than that would cause her dismissal. And I insisted she finish the project. She proudly told me it was done and on my desk.

It was, but it was wrong. I explained to her again how to do it right, my confidence in her sorely flagging. She explained that she'd told her boyfriend not to call her, that she would call him and only once a day. Somewhat mollified, I went back to work.

After lunch, her boyfriend called twice. Each time she was on the phone for fifteen minutes or more. I was watching her now. I took her outside the office.

I gave Brittany my list of grievances, and she broke into tears. But, she left within the hour.

Sometimes, you just have to cut the cord. Women are not socialized in our culture to hire and fire in most cases. Especially not in social matters like shower planning. But if any member of your team is causing you stress or stressing the rest of the team by stupid behavior, and with one frank discussion you do not see immediate improvement, as the party manager, it's your job to cut them loose.

handle it before it causes hard feelings that spill into animosities at your shower.

If one person is picking a fight with another cohost or helper, see if you can arrange for them to work separately by shifting their tasks or the times they do what they need to do. If they are both engaged in random shelling, you can probably solve it by sitting down with both of them and adjudicating the situation as if they were fighting children. The bottom line is, the responsibilities were divided at the first meeting. There's no reason for anyone to be stepping into others' arenas. Remind them both that they volunteered to do this because they love the mother-to-be and that their behavior is annoying to everyone and will disrupt the party. Ach, children!

Solving Problem (e) "Agreeing to Do Something One Way and Then Doing It Differently Anyway"

There could be three reasons for this:

1. You weren't clear in your directions.
2. The other person didn't understand your directions.
3. The other person doesn't agree with your directions.

For one or two, be more simple and clear and specific. For number three, sit down with her in a neutral setting and ask her why she didn't do it the way she had said she would. You may discover a very good reason. Otherwise, you may need to ask her to do it over the way it was planned, and if she refuses or cannot, then perhaps you should suggest you reassign the balance of her duties to someone else, but leave her as a cohost on the invitations.

Solving Problem (f) "Other Annoying Things That Make You Wish You Could Dump Her"

If she's really driving you nuts and you cannot take any more, you may indeed have to dump her. (See the sidebar about Brittany.) But if she's simply pesky or calls too often to ask you questions or seems to have no life except participating in the shower, the first best bet is direct communication.

> *You: Elizabeth, I really appreciate your enthusiasm for this baby shower, but I've got to tell you that the way you always call me at 3 a.m. with new ideas is driving me crazy.*
> *Elizabeth the Pest: Well, you said if we had ideas we could call you!*
> *You: Elizabeth, I like your ideas. But the shower is a week away, and I don't have time to think about any more ideas. Why don't you write them down so if we ever do another baby shower in the future, we can use them? But you have to stop calling me at 3 a.m. It's disrupting my sleep, and I feel angry when I hear the phone ringing then . . .*

Therapists always tell us to tell other people how their behavior makes us feel in an "I" story: I feel *X* when you act in *Y* fashion." It gives the other person a chance to consider the effect of their behavior on others.

OK, this wasn't meant to be a management textbook, but this is important. A baby shower isn't like planning a wedding or the high school prom. But it can get nutty at the last minute if people aren't working as a team.

How Do I Properly Acknowledge Everyone Who Helps Me?

With the exception of a party you cohost with someone else (in which case both of your names would appear on the invitation as the hostesses), the best and easiest way to thank the people who help you is loudly and in public at the shower. Check this probable scenario out:

You are now named Martha . . .
"Oh, Martha! That's a lovely cake!" says Gertrude.

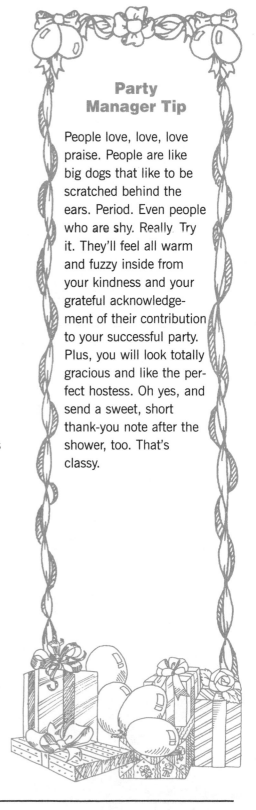

Party Manager Tip

People love, love, love praise. People are like big dogs that like to be scratched behind the ears. Period. Even people who are shy. Really. Try it. They'll feel all warm and fuzzy inside from your kindness and your grateful acknowledgement of their contribution to your successful party. Plus, you will look totally gracious and like the perfect hostess. Oh yes, and send a sweet, short thank-you note after the shower, too. That's classy.

You say, "Oh yes, isn't it amazing? Pam actually baked and decorated it herself. Can you believe how great she did?" Smiling at Pam, you introduce her to Gertrude if they don't know one another.

You are now the greatest hostess in the world. See? They both think you are gracious and charming and charitable. (OK, now you can go back to your regular name.)

Minding the Phone

There is one commonly known secret to all entertaining: The last few hours before the event, the phone will ring with a bunch of insanely trivial questions. It's guaranteed. If you're as sweet as apple pie, you can pick it up every time and kindly tell the callers what they need to know. Me, I don't do sweet, but you already know that from reading this book.

Now, call me evil but I never have time for all the calls before a party. And the reasons for calling always seem silly. And I'm always busy, as you'll probably be. So here are my suggestions for handling these unwelcome last-minute "emergency" phone calls.

1. Get an official phone answerer—like a teenage kid. Have them answer the questions and deal with the results, and not disturb you unless it's major.

2. Put your answering machine on and screen the calls. Change your outgoing message to state "Hi, this is Shellie. I'm getting ready for Cindy's wedding shower right now, and I cannot answer the phone. If you are calling about the shower, it's from 7:30 to 9 P.M., dress is casual, dinner will be served. The address is 213 Maple Drive, just south of Canyon View off Westcott Road. It's OK if you are going to be a little late, if

you want to bring someone, or if you cannot make it at the last minute. Leave a message and let me know what's up with you. Everybody else can leave a message, too."

Think about it: How likely is it that the stalker your mom warned you about when you moved out on your own will be randomly dialing answering machines and get your number and address and crash the party? Not very. It's much more likely 99 percent of the calls you get during the three hours that this is your outgoing message will be from people who are related somehow to the party!

Dealing with Emergencies

Just like the Boy Scouts always say, "Be prepared!" Flat tires, people choking, someone throws up on your carpet, she goes into labor while there, your kid gets the flu that morning, aaarrrgggh! These things happen.

First of all, emotionally prepare yourself that anything can happen. The worst attitude I think you can have is "This has to be perfect." Reality check! Nobody's perfect. Most people will have a really great time and be totally oblivious to things that go wrong. It's like a wedding or any other party. It never goes exactly as planned, and stressing out won't help.

In the case of medical emergencies, of course you'd dial 911. Brush up on the Heimlich maneuver, too, just in case. Have some local guy on call in case someone gets a flat tire or locks her keys in her car or something—not that you cannot take care of it, but it's going to take one more responsibility off your plate. Be prepared to find a replacement babysitter at the last minute for your kid(s).

Who Should Arrive First?

Depending on your situation, the mother-to-be or the guests should arrive first. If it's a surprise shower, you obviously already can answer this question.

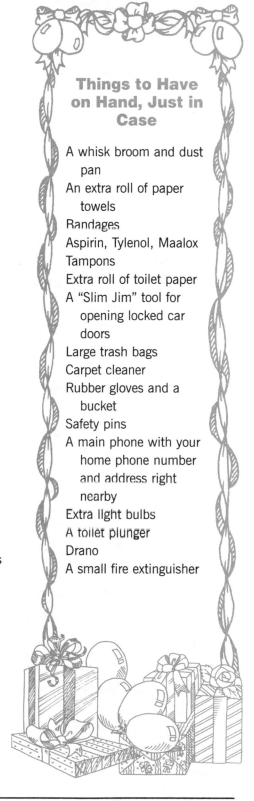

Things to Have on Hand, Just in Case

A whisk broom and dust pan
An extra roll of paper towels
Bandages
Aspirin, Tylenol, Maalox
Tampons
Extra roll of toilet paper
A "Slim Jim" tool for opening locked car doors
Large trash bags
Carpet cleaner
Rubber gloves and a bucket
Safety pins
A main phone with your home phone number and address right nearby
Extra light bulbs
A toilet plunger
Drano
A small fire extinguisher

Countdown to the Party!

Six Weeks Before:

❑ Ask the father- or mother-to-be how he or she feels about you hosting it, and if you should have anyone else cohost it with you.

❑ Contact your potential cohosts.

❑ Have a planning and delegation meeting with your cohosts.

❑ Determine your budget.

❑ Select location, date, and time.

❑ Decide on theme.

❑ Get list of possible attendees' addresses.

❑ Go buy party goods or at least invitations, unless you make them by hand.

One Month Before:

❑ Input names and addresses into your computer.

❑ Mail invitations to your potential attendees.

❑ Order the cake.

❑ Select a menu.

❑ Interview caterers.

❑ Hire a caterer.

Two Weeks Before:

❑ Make first RSVP calls to stragglers.

❑ Start buying nonperishable food items.

❑ Buy the last-minute decorations.

❑ Call a local maid service and invest $40 in your sanity by buying after-party cleanup help. (It's pointless to do it before!)

One Week Before:

- ❑ Confirm the cake.
- ❑ Confirm the caterer.
- ❑ Confirm the room.
- ❑ Make last RSVP calls.
- ❑ Make the party favors.
- ❑ Call to confirm the schedule with any entertainers you have hired.

The Day Before:

- ❑ Hang the decorations (but not paper streamers!).
- ❑ Make the ice flower bouquets.
- ❑ Prepare advance food.
- ❑ Do any baking.
- ❑ Buy any perishable grocery items.
- ❑ Make sure you have at least three rolls of film and good flash batteries.
- ❑ Make sure you have spare light bulbs.
- ❑ Set up any games you will be playing.

The Morning Of:

- ❑ Frost the cake and refrigerate it when you're done.
- ❑ Get out every single serving utensil you will use and lay them out.
- ❑ Set the tables, including the gift table.
- ❑ Wash a head of romaine lettuce to garnish trays of food with.
- ❑ Wash a bunch of parsley for the same reason.
- ❑ Arrange, pick up, or have the flowers delivered.
- ❑ Finish the decorating.

Two Hours Before:

- ❑ Blow up the balloons.
- ❑ Finish the major cooking.
- ❑ Set up the buffet table
- ❑ Put two or three stems of flowers in a bud vase in your bathroom.
- ❑ Put a pad and pen on the chair of the person who will sit to the mother-to-be's right during gift opening.
- ❑ Clean the litter box, spray air freshener.

One Hour Before:

- ❑ Make sure your bathroom is sparkling clean.
- ❑ Put an extra roll of toilet paper in an obvious but discreet place.
- ❑ Go put on a nice outfit and do your makeup again.

Fifteen Minutes Before:

- ❑ Add ice to the punch.
- ❑ Put the cake on the table.
- ❑ Light the candles.
- ❑ Straighten up your kitchen.
- ❑ Turn on the music—unless you hired somebody.
- ❑ Put Kitty or Rover away so he doesn't get scared by guests or cause any problems.

It's wonderful if you have a mother-to-be who is willing to arrive a half-hour early to help you with the last-minute stuff. She can also greet people as they come (some of whom are probably total strangers to you) and introduce people to one another. But she doesn't have to do this, of course, and probably won't want to if she's already stressed to the max from planning for the baby, or if she isn't the very social type.

Otherwise, your guests should be scheduled to arrive half an hour before the mother-to-be. This way, latecomers still are there in time when the mother-to-be walks in, and when the mother-to-be gets there, she sees a huge pile of presents neatly arranged on the table you've decorated, waiting for her. She also walks into a room full of friends, which is a very nice feeling.

What Do We Do During the Shower?

The main events of a shower are eating and unwrapping gifts. You can add party games or some other activity if you want, and you can add dancing for a coed shower. If it's a surprise party, the other main event is seeing the mother-to-be's surprise when she walks in.

Do We Eat Before or After the Gifts Are Opened?

Ah, here you get to use your discretion! If you've got lots of people and thus zillions of presents to open, and you've scheduled this near a mealtime, you'll have hungry, bored guests watching the mother-to-be open the mountain of presents. But if you feed them before, people will be juggling cake plates on their laps while they are trying to ooh and aah and maybe even pass for inspection the lovely gifts you all bring her.

At my first baby shower, we ate cake after the gifts were opened, and one guest was horrified at this departure from what she perceived as custom.

I'll Never Forget Ol' What's-Her-Name!

If your guests don't know each other, you should provide name tags. There's nothing worse than Elizabeth having a twenty-minute conversation with Janet, and then at the end, neither one knows the other's name.

Get a package of name tags. Get a huge Magic Marker and write everyone's name on it. If you want to be artsy, use glitter glue. Have the tags by the door so that as people come in and you or the mother-to-be greets them, you can stick it onto their dresses—and be wearing one yourself. Since everyone will know your mother-to-be, make hers elaborate with bits of lace and ribbons, and simply say "Mother-to-be" on it.

Figure it this way. If you're personally going to be stressed out that something will be too hot or cold if you open gifts first, because you are catering it yourself or doing it potluck, then eat first. If you think it's going to be a bother to have plates and glasses all over your house when people are hanging around watching her open gifts, then eat later. Especially if you're worried about spills. Or you could serve hors d'oeuvres before and the meal after. Make this part easy on yourself, and damn the etiquette torpedoes.

CHAPTER 11

Great Shower Activities

Being a hostess can be fun. In the words of my dear friend Amy, the goal of any party is for the hostess to walk in and have fun, and the details to take care of themselves. This is going to happen only with careful planning, which is something you have done as you worked through this book.

As hostess, you not only want to have fun, you want to make sure your mother-to-be has lots and lots of fun, and your guests do, too. You want it to be enjoyable, comfortable, and memorable. This is easy. You just have to work from the opposite perspective: The deal is, you have to make sure you don't make anyone feel uncomfortable.

Following Your Theme

If you've chosen a theme from this book, chances are there's a shower game that's perfect for it, and it was mentioned in the theme description. There may be other games that would be perfect for the type of girls you and your mother-to-be are.

Let the Games Begin

Games can be loads of fun at parties! They break the ice, heat up the conversation and get guests actively involved. There are games obviously related to the party theme, and then there are traditional shower games.

Some games include:

Pin the Diaper on the Baby: In this game you use a big picture of a baby on a corkboard and a white washcloth or men's handkerchief. Blindfold the guests, spin them around twice, and they try to pin the diaper on the baby's butt.

Baby Trivial Pursuit: Collect a bunch of trivia about babies. Write the questions on the front and the answers on the back of 3" × 5" cards. Separate your guests into two groups, each with at least ten cards. Make sure parents and nonparents are evenly dispersed! Have each side quiz the other, one question at a time. The team that has the most right answers, wins!

Herstory: You write out a humorous story, in advance of the shower, preferably on one of those large newsprint flip charts. (They cost about $2 at the arts and crafts store.) You leave blanks for some of the nouns, verbs, and adjectives. At the party, you fill in the story with the words guests call out to you to create a funny story about the mother-to-be and new daddy and their life with the new baby.

Lucky Girl: On the bottom of the paper cups in which beverages will be served, write the mother-to-be's name, new daddy's name, and other baby-related words (diaper, bottle, pacifier, crib, etc.). Put all the words on matching slips of paper. The mother-to-be picks one slip of paper out of a hat or jar during the party. Whoever has that particular word on the bottom of her cup wins a small prize.

Doing a Funny Skit: If anyone in your set can write, sing, dance or act, or if anyone should have been a comedian and missed her calling, why not put together these talented folks and create a special ten- or fifteen-minute skit for shower? Steal ideas from Letterman, Leno or Raphael, or make up something totally your own.

Memories Activity: Have everyone bring a photo of the mother-to-be or new daddy or herself with the mother-to-be. Assemble them into a montage. Write on the back where each one was taken, and the memory associated with it. Or collect written memories and put them in a memory book for the mother-to-be, with or without the pictures.

Baby Care Manual: Have all the mothers on the guest list write out their suggestions for great mothering, collect poems about mothers, mothering, babies, and stuff like that. Lay it out in a gorgeous scrapbook with pressed flowers and pictures of babies. Have her own mother write a short piece about being a mother, or a poem. Make it a real keepsake!

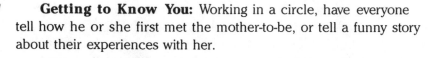

Getting to Know You: Working in a circle, have everyone tell how he or she first met the mother-to-be, or tell a funny story about their experiences with her.

Baby Diapering Game: For this game you need a pile of newborn diapers, four life-size dolls, and four packages of baby wipes. Split your group into four, or if there are only twelve women, two teams. On the mark, the first person in line must change the baby's diaper, including wiping its bottom and putting on a clean diaper. Next in line begins as soon as she/he finishes, and so on until everyone on the team has changed the baby. The winning team gets to go through the buffet line first for cake!

Baby Sucking Game: Fill six bottles (or so) with juice or milk. Get six (or more) volunteers, who have to compete by sucking the baby bottle dry. Whoever finishes the bottle first, wins.

Dirty Diaper Door Prize: Buy a package of cotton or disposable diapers, enough so that there's one for each guest. In one of the diapers, put a big glob of something like seeded mustard or peanut butter. Fold up all the diapers, including the dirty one. Put all the diapers in a bag. Each person has to remove a diaper from the bag. The one who gets the dirty diaper gets a door prize.

Baby Bingo: In advance, prepare enough bingo cards so each guest can have one. Draw five vertical and five horizontal squares with a dark marker on a sheet of paper. Copy them. At the party, have your guests write down the names of items they think the mother-to-be will get as baby gifts. (They can include each item only once.) Then, pass out stickers with a baby motif OR give everyone a pen during the present opening. The first one to get bingo gets a door prize.

This Baby Is Driving Me Nuts! Get a life-sized doll that can have its clothes and diapers changed. Each guest gets a chance to take the fully dressed baby, strip it, change it, and replace its clothes. However, while she or he is doing that, the other guests create typical stay-at-home-Mom distractions. They can do everything except touch the contestant above the waist. (Which means they can pretend to be the three-year-old big sister who's just fallen and scraped her knee.) Each guest can be something different—the phone ringing, the UPS man, the dog vomiting on the couch, the oven catching on fire, the fire alarm going off, someone knocking on the back door, etc. The contestant must complete the task despite all these distractions in the background. Use a timer to find out which of you is able to handle the baby and the emergencies most efficiently. The one with the shortest time is the winner. Contestants CANNOT leave the baby unattended to roll off the table, and they must respond to all cries for help as though they were real. The same problems must occur for each contestant.

Mystery Guest: This is a neat twist on a boring old party game. Arrange to have someone show up at the party, in the middle of the festivities, as a crasher. Your crasher must be someone the guests don't know. Make the person dress odd and act weird, and her or she should be carrying a large satchel.

As the hostess, you loudly ask the crasher's name. You ask if her or she knows the mother-to-be. The guest says, "Huh, sure," rather uncertainly. Everyone will think your baby shower has just been crashed! Sternly tell the visitor you must see his or her invitation. The mystery guest plops down right there on the floor and begins unloading baby things from his or her large satchel or backpack.

Surely this event will have everyone's attention. Have the crasher unload the satchel piece by piece, allegedly looking for the lost invitation, which is finally the last item removed from the bag. You accept it slowly, as the person is putting everything quickly back into the bag.

Then, turn to your guests, announce who this person really is, and ask everyone to take a piece of paper and write down every object in the person's satchel. The one who can remember the most, wins. At the end, take everything out again—it's now a gift for the expectant mom.

This Little Piggy Goes to Market: Buy an empty piggy bank for the new baby and place it on your coffee table for this game. Ask all your guests to pull out their pocket change. (Have

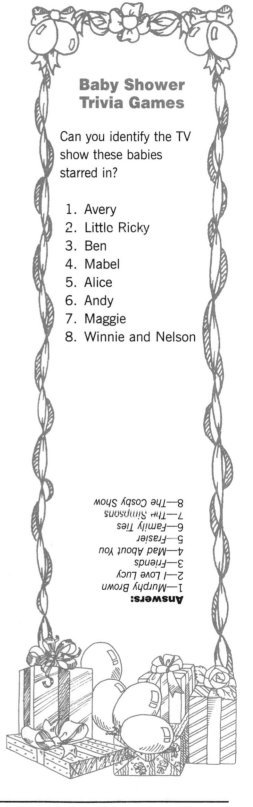

Baby Shower Trivia Games

Can you identify the TV show these babies starred in?

1. Avery
2. Little Ricky
3. Ben
4. Mabel
5. Alice
6. Andy
7. Maggie
8. Winnie and Nelson

Answers:
1—Murphy Brown
2—I Love Lucy
3—Friends
4—Mad About You
5—Frasier
6—Family Ties
7—The Simpsons
8—The Cosby Show

some on hand just in case someone doesn't have any with them.) Going around the room, beginning with you, state something you have never done. (I've never bungee jumped, I've never flown a plane, etc.) Then, each guest who HAS done what you've never done has to put a coin in the piggy bank. If the bank isn't full enough, go around twice. Otherwise, once everyone is done—you give the piggy bank to the mother as the baby's first piggy bank with money.

Mary, Mary, Quite Contrary: This charming game is a real stumper! Open up a nursery-rhyme book before the game and select phrases from the rhymes. Make up at least two per person for as many people as you expect (e.g., write thirty if you expect fifteen women). Give all your guests a sheet of paper and a pen. Read the line aloud, as in, "The sheep's in the meadow." Without saying it aloud, each guest must write the title of the rhyme from which the line is derived in the first space on her paper. Repeat until you've used all the rhyme snippets you collected. Have a list of answers, that is, the names of the rhymes. Whoever has the most correct is the winner.

Birth Records: Buy a bunch of little plastic babies, at least one per person. Freeze them in an ice cube tray filled with pink and blue water (use food coloring). Each guest gets a baby ice cube in her drink when she arrives. They have to say precisely when their baby will be born. Write all estimates down on pieces of paper. The baby is born the moment it is free of the ice entirely (no cheating by sucking on it, putting it under hot tap water, etc.). The winner is the one who guesses closest when his or her baby will be born.

The Price Is Right Game: Buy a dozen baby items of various prices (like a can of wipes, some Desitin, a jar of baby food, a box of Zwieback, a pacifier, etc.). On little slips of paper, or 3" × 5" cards, write precisely what you paid for each item. Seal the papers in envelopes, but keep a master list for yourself. As the emcee, you choose the contestants by randomly drawing their name from a box. (You can have your guests write their names on slips of paper when they walk in.) Or you can have the mother-to-be draw the names. Choose three contestants at a time, and just as on the game show *The Price is Right*, have them guess on five of the objects. The ones closest to the exact price win the index cards. Then, play with three more contestants. The one with the most index cards wins!

This Is Your Life! Having a "This Is Your Life!" shower would be loads of fun if your guests include family and friends who may not know each other. Get each of your guests who RSVPs to tell you their favorite anecdote about the mother-to-be. Ask for pictures. Call her mom and get background information such as when she was born, the type of labor mom had, and so forth.

If you've got dramatic flair, tape-record a baby crying as your intro, with "It's a girl!" as a voice-over. Continue with a "Jennifer Sexton—(drum roll)—This is your life!" Then, emcee a wonderful journey through the bride's life. To make it even more fun, try to invite her best friend from out of town (high school) whom she hasn't talked to in years, or the mother-to-be's sister from Georgia who told her she couldn't make it, or anyone else you think your mother-to-be would go nuts to see. If you cannot get a relative or an old friend, why not hire her favorite author (authors eat up this type of chance to be a big star! You'll have to pay air-fare, though, and a night's lodging). Try getting her favorite English teacher from grammar school, someone like that. Do some investi-gating to find out whom she'd most love to see. Put him or her up at your house if you have to.

If you are going to do this, play it not more than thirty minutes into the shower, so the surprise guest gets to enjoy the party, too, and not just wait in the wings, and so that the late guests (there are always a few) won't miss the fun.

Baby Pins in a Bottle: Fill a jar with brightly colored diaper pins, jelly beans, or small candies, and have each guest write down her best estimate. The winner who is closest to the true number wins a prize!

Mother's Circumference: This is a traditional baby shower game. Get a skein of baby yarn in pink, blue, and yellow and you'll need a pair of scissors, too. Pass the yarn around and have each guest estimate how much string it will take to fit around the mother-to-be's tummy at the navel. Then, the mom-to-be has to try on each person's string. The closest one that fits, wins!

Pin Your Lips Shut! Ouch! Upon arrival, guests are given a diaper pin to attach to their clothes. They are told the one word no one can mention—will it be "baby"? The mother-to-be's name? The word "crib" or "diaper" or something else? Pick something your guests will likely be talking about at the shower. And then whenever anyone says it, they have to give their pin to the person who caught them. The person with the most pins at the end of the gift opening is the winner.

The Baby Food Game: OK, this is a traditional but revolting game that will make you want to spit your food into someone's face and soil your bib. Buy a variety of baby foods, say six to eight jars, including some nasty ones like strained beets with oatmeal. (Yucko!) Write down the brand and the flavor of the baby food for each jar. Rip the labels off each one and replace them with numbers marked on stickers or masking tape swatches. Make sure your numbers correspond to the labels you removed. Open the jars before the party and arrange them on a little taster tray. (A box lid will do fine.) Each willing guest has to take a tiny taste of each one and guess what flavor it is and who made it (Gerber, Earth's Best, etc.). The guest who gets the most FLAVORS right wins, the guest who gets the most MANUFACTURERS right wins another prize! And we feed this stuff to babies and wonder why they spit it back?

Baby Pictures Game: Have each guest bring her baby picture. (Mention it in the invitation!) Number and arrange all the pictures on a big corkboard (without poking holes through them). Let each guest try to figure out who is who. Of course, you cannot simply take the photo straight from the hand of the woman who just walked in and hang it on the board—that's too obvious. Instead, collect and hang half a dozen at a time. (Keep a log of them as they come in so you know which number matches which guest.) Then, have each guest guess, by number, which baby is which guest. The winner is the one who guesses the most correctly.

Celebrity Baby Pictures: For variety, you might be able to scrounge up some celebrity baby pictures on the Web, in biographies, or elsewhere. Mingle them in with the game above, or make them into a game of their own.

How to Hire Any Talent

Hiring someone to entertain your mother-to-be and your guests at the party is always fun, although it may be a bit pricey. If you don't know anyone who will give you a cutrate or who would do it for free because they are a friend, you'll have to hire someone.

First, figure out what would work best for your location and the type of guests you are having and when you are having the shower. Then, look in the Yellow Pages under the appropriate word. (Some newspapers' Classifieds sections might offer help, too.) Call no less than six places—the ones with the half-page Yellow Pages ads will be more expensive than the one with the fine print that says, "Margie's Trained Animal Act and Hair Salon." Make a selection.

Again, if the person who answers the phone is a jerk, or rude, find another place to call. Get prices from six people. Tell them your party date, what the event is, and ask what they provide for your money. Ask them to send you a brochure and a referral list. I might hire someone who didn't have a brochure (probably because they'd be cheaper), but I would NEVER hire someone who couldn't provide me with a list of satisfied customers!

Narrow it down to two or three, and go see the performer live. Ask them if you can crash their next gig for ten minutes, or if you can have a demo tape, or whatever. Somehow, make sure they can do what they are promising and that you aren't the first person who is buying from them. Not much is worse than a really bad entertainer. Your guests will be trapped!

From there, you can probably make a good choice all by yourself. It's customary to put down 50 percent to hold the date. Remember to confirm the engagement a few days before the party. If they don't show, have a backup of one of the games in this book—and get your money back.

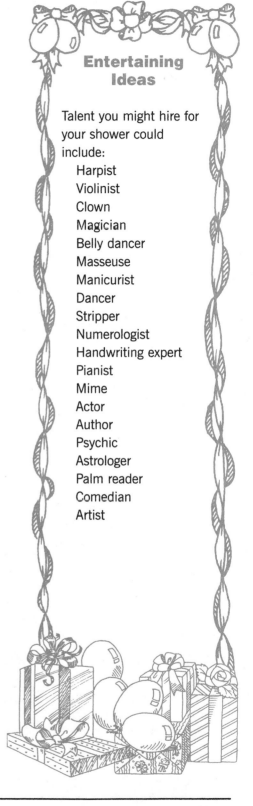

Entertaining Ideas

Talent you might hire for your shower could include:
Harpist
Violinist
Clown
Magician
Belly dancer
Masseuse
Manicurist
Dancer
Stripper
Numerologist
Handwriting expert
Pianist
Mime
Actor
Author
Psychic
Astrologer
Palm reader
Comedian
Artist

Hire a Local Parenting or Childbirth Author

I'm partial to this idea for a number of reasons. To find a local author, call your biggest local bookstore and ask if they know someone. Call the local branch of PEN if you are in a big city, or look under "Publisher's Representatives" or "Literary Agents" in the Yellow Pages. These people probably know someone. Short of that, call the local library. There's bound to be someone. Get this person in to read a bit from their book, offer them some cake. If you want them to do it for free, tell them you'll put the book on display and/or let them sell copies afterward. Authors are natural-born hams for the most part, especially those who write on these topics. And the best part? You get an amusing diversion for free!

Hiring a Palm Reader, Astrologer, or Psychic

What an incredibly trendy and fun twist to your shower! If you don't know anyone who does this kind of thing, ask around! One of your friends is bound to be able to give you a recommendation. After you get the recommendation, go visit this person yourself! Yep, get a reading. See what you think about them. Then ask them if they would be willing to do the shower. Chances are strong the answer will be yes, as most of these professionals don't make a lot of money.

Write up a short contract that says, "Zelda the Magnificent will attend a baby shower at (location) on (date, time) and perform readings for all who wish it, not to exceed (number of) people. In deference to this contract, I make a deposit of $75 [I wouldn't put down more than that!] toward this event, the balance of $(agreed-on remainder) to be paid at the completion of the party." You sign it and have her do the same. Don't take chances. My experience with the majority of these professionals is they spend a lot of time living in other universes and aren't always great about contracts and things. Call a few days before and also the day of the shower to be sure.

Make sure you set up a private room for Zelda to do the readings in, and have your guests pencil in the time of their reading when they arrive.

Hiring an Impersonator

From Mae West to Abe Lincoln to Barbara Walters to the president, good and bad impersonators are everywhere. Think of all the *Saturday Night Live* skits you've seen! An impersonator may be just the right touch for your event. To hire one, call a local speakers' bureau, or you can find any impersonator you want by calling ForthWrite Speakers Bureau (my agent's company) in Malibu, California, at 310-457-5785. The impersonator can show up in person, or just do it over the phone.

How to Hire a Male Dancer/Stripper

While this may be the domain of the bachelorette party, you might choose to do it at the baby shower, assuming you won't freak out any of the guests. How do you find the right guy? First, look in the Yellow Pages under "Dancers." (Some Classifieds sections will offer this, too.) Call no less than six places—the ones with the half-page Yellow Pages ads will be more expensive than the one with the fine print that says, "Joe's Male Strippers and TV Repair Shop." Make a selection.

If the person who answers the phone is a jerk, or rude, find another place to call. Get prices from six people. Tell them your party date, what the event is, and ask what they provide. (Own music? More than ten minutes of dancing? Any interaction with the guest of honor?)

Narrow it down to two or three, and go see the guys who will actually be stripping/dancing. From there, you can probably make a good choice all by yourself. Remember to confirm his engagement a few days before the party.

Take Them Dancing

It wouldn't be totally out of place to organize your baby shower around something interesting, like a group dancing lesson. If you think the mom-to-be is up to it, you could drag everyone down to the local Arthur Murray studio (after the cake and presents) and let them all learn how to cha-cha.

Poker, Bridge, Card Games

Why not set up card-game tables for your guests? Could you enjoy playing elimination rounds and offering a prize to the winner? Instead of betting with money, you could bet with X number of plastic baby things from the crafts store. A small crib is worth ten points, for example, but a tiny plastic baby bottle only two.

Charades

People just don't play charades often enough anymore, if you want my opinion. What a great game! In case you're a bit rusty, this hilarious game is played by organizing your guests into two teams.

Each team member writes down one idea on a strip of paper. Since it's a baby shower, it could be something related to babies. Or Disney characters. Or something like that. Otherwise, movies, animals, famous people, and words are all typical choices. Each team's strips of paper are put into a hat.

The opposite team offers the person whose turn it is on the other team a chance to draw one slip of paper from their hat. Let's say the paper says "baby carriage." The person now has to coax his or her team members into saying the words "baby carriage" without using any words.

To refer to "sounds like" he or she can pull on his or her ear. To refer to how many letters are in the word, or how many words, hold up fingers.

The person has a maximum of five minutes to evoke the word from his or her teammates. If she or he can do it, it's a point for that team.

Then, it's the opposite team's turn to offer up one of their teammates to choose a word from the other team's hat. People can pass on performing, but they must stay active in helping solve the words!

Indian Summer

I have absolutely no idea why this game is called Indian Summer, because it has nothing to do with either. But it is interesting and can be funny. All the guests sit in a large circle so each can see the faces of the others.

In unison, all persons present must slap their legs two times (slap! slap!), then clap their hands two times (clap! clap!), and then snap their fingers, first left, then right (snap! snap!). So the game goes slap-slap-clap-clap-snap-snap.

Repeat the rhythm a half-dozen times for everyone to get the movement. It's pretty basic. The first person to go says a word on the left snap of their fingers and the name of a person on the right snap. As in, "slap-slap-clap-clap-diaper-Brenda" (at nonbaby showers, any related word will do to start).

Brenda must pick up the verbal ball without stopping the motion of slap-slap. When she gets to left snap, she has to say a word associated with "diaper." On the right snap, she has to say the name of anyone else in the circle. Here's a sample. For slap . . . I use SSCC.

First player: SSCC—diaper—Brenda

Brenda: SSCC—diaper pin—Paul (a diaper needs pins)

Paul: SSCC—rectal thermometer—Linda (both cover the same area)

Linda: SSCC—pacifier—Gina (both are inserted into baby's orifices)

And so on. The humor in this game comes from the speed at which one must think not only of someone's name but of a word association for what they were just given. I've been part of this game a dozen times, and it can be hilarious.

Again, it has nothing to do with Indians or summer. Go figure!

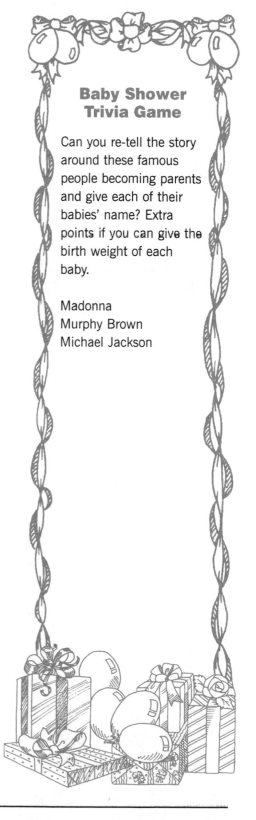

Baby Shower Trivia Game

Can you re-tell the story around these famous people becoming parents and give each of their babies' name? Extra points if you can give the birth weight of each baby.

Madonna
Murphy Brown
Michael Jackson

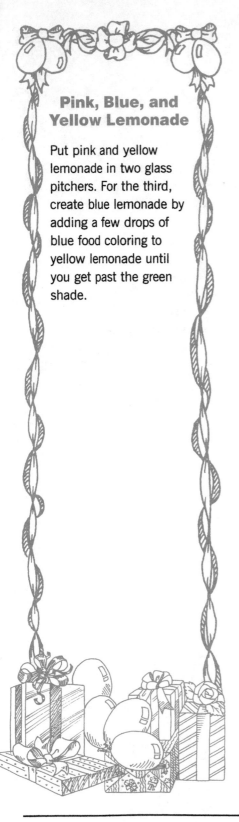

Pink, Blue, and Yellow Lemonade

Put pink and yellow lemonade in two glass pitchers. For the third, create blue lemonade by adding a few drops of blue food coloring to yellow lemonade until you get past the green shade.

The Dictionary Game

As a kid, this was one of my family's favorites. Get a pile of scratch paper and pens, and a serious dictionary. That's all you need. Pass out paper and pens. The first person opens the dictionary and asks if anyone in the room knows the definition of the word she has randomly chosen off that page. You could try to make it all about baby words, but for that you'd need the pediatric desk reference.

If no one does, that is the word for this round of the game. The woman holding the dictionary tells the guests how to spell the word. Then the guests write down a plausible or silly definition for the word, the best they can. Of course, none of them will get it right. The person who is holding the dictionary chooses one of the definitions listed for that word, and she writes it down, too. The guests write their names on the bottom of their slips of paper and pass them all to the player with the dictionary. She mixes them up, and, in random order, reads them by number. Number 1, name of the word, definition. When she has read them all, going around the room, each person gets to vote by number for the most likely definition of the word.

She tracks the voting by saying, "How many vote for Number 1?" When the voting guests raise their hands, that's how many points are given to the writer of that definition, whomever that may have been. And so on, through all the chosen definitions. (Some will not be voted for at all.)

At the end, she announces which was the REAL definition. If no one voted for it, she gets a point for every person in the room. Otherwise, like every other player, she gets only as many points as people voted for her definition, but the people who guessed correctly get five points each. The dictionary and score card passes clockwise.

Get a Piñata!

A piñata is a hollow papier-mâché object, often made to look like a person or animal. You can get them at the party store, or if you live in a neighborhood with a Hispanic section, you can buy a better one there for probably one third what you'd pay at the party store.

Getting Prizes Donated to Your Shower

This might take a bit of pluck, but you certainly have that by now! To get prizes donated, decide what you want. A buy-one-get-one-free dinner from a local restaurant? A free soda with a to-go lunch order from the deli on the corner? A free dozen donuts? Ten dollars off from the lingerie store? All you gotta do is call a couple of small, independent retailers in your area and you'll have prizes coming out of your ears!

Pitch it like this, in person, to the manager or owner:

"Hi, my name is Gloria. I'm hosting a party for one of my friends who is having a baby. We'll be having about twenty local women. I've always loved your corned-beef-and-peanut-butter-on-rye sandwiches here, so I was thinking, Wouldn't it be fun if you offered a free one to someone who wins one of the party games? You'd come

to the attention of all twenty women, and maybe expand a little business. Who knows? Whoever wins the CB&PB on rye might get as addicted as I am and become a regular. Whaddya say?"

They'll likely say one of the following: Yes!; Well, how about a free Coke if they buy the sandwich instead; or No, honey, but here's a french fry for your troubles. It's easy! When she or he says yes, pull out the preprinted gift certificate (their store's name nicely pre-printed with the address) and write on the blank line what they are providing. Have them sign it and give it an expiration date (six months is perfect). Great! Now you have a valuable prize that didn't cost you more than a few pennies!

Or, think of which attendees have their own businesses and get them to donate something. Retail stores especially love this kind of opportunity.

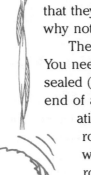

The deal with piñatas, which are de rigeur at kids' parties, is that they are fun. The adults watch kids wistfully at kids' parties, so why not make one for your adults' party?

The piñata is filled with wrapped candy and/or little surprises. You need not fill the whole thing, just at least half. The opening is sealed (usually with Elmer's glue!) and the piñata is hung at the end of a long rope. The rope is then slung over a tree limb, creating a sort of pulley with the piñata on one end. When the rope is pulled, the piñata slides up and down in space and wiggles around. You will want to have someone managing the rope-pulling during this game.

When the guests are ready, you line them up shortest to tallest. You blindfold the first one and give her a baseball bat. She's supposed to hit the moving piñata and bust it open, spilling the contents. She gets three swings. If she doesn't crack open the swaying piñata, the bat and blindfold go to the next woman. And so on.

Don't play this game if you have men at your shower—they get way too competitive and nutty. But women might think it's fun. When the thing is finally hit hard enough to crack open, the candy/small gift items/tiny perfume samples, whatever you filled it with, spill out and the idea is everyone is supposed to scramble for the contents.

Getting grown women to scramble for the contents might be a little hard, so before the game, announce you've put a special copper penny into one candy wrapper and whoever finds it wins . . . a prize? An all-expense-paid lunch for two with the mother-to-be? Your choice!

Conducting a Raffle

A raffle or two can be lots of fun at a shower. Pick out one or two funny, cute, or pretty prizes, usually not exceeding $20 each in cost. I always suggest plants. You can also collect some trivial prizes— plastic blow horns and funny party hats. Make some sort of a system whereby guests can win.

Or, base your raffle on something besides luck. Who knows the mother-to-be's grandma's native country? Who knows the new daddy's middle name? Or give prizes to the winners of the games we've just talked about.

Prizes—What to Get

There are a million things you can buy for door prizes and contest winners. I suggest a trip to your local super deep discount/remainders store. You can get some pretty awesome stuff for not a whole lot of dough.

If you're handy, try one of these great ideas:

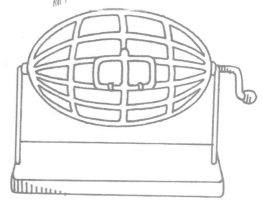

- Paint a new clay pot (any size) white.
- Sponge paint some of the pot in a contrasting color. (You can use more than one color if you like!)
- Plant a little plant in it, tie it with a bow, and you've got a prize.

Or, remember those amazing loop potholders we made as kids? Remember how our mothers swore those were the best potholders in the world? Guess what? Those kits are all over the stores now, complete with loops, for about $3. Make a couple of potholders, but don't make them ugly like we did when we were kids!

If you have a pair of needle-nose pliers and a good eye, trot down to your local bead shop. You'd be amazed at all the ideas you'll get for making simple, cute, or elegant jewelry easily and inexpensively.

You can give a coupon to perform a service. You can give products the company you own or work for creates (if you can buy at an employee discount or talk your boss into a donation!). You can give simple things like a loaf of home-baked bread, or something elaborate like a floral arrangement you made yourself with real or fake flowers. The list of possible door prizes and the cleverness you apply to this task are all that are stopping you. You could even implore your cohosts or other guests to pitch in to come up with clever door prizes—does one of them knit coasters or Barbie dresses? Does the mother-to-be's grandmother want to do something but all she knows how to do is crochet? The sky's the limit!

Let Them Eat Cake!

In summary of all these activities, themes, games, party ideas, raffles, and what not, it really is about your friend who is about to have a baby. It's about celebrating and supporting her as she prepares to bring a precious new life into the world, and making her feel like she has a team of loving friends supporting her and sharing in her bliss. If you want to, just put on some nice music, gather a group of friends, and let them eat cake!

Taking Great Pictures of the Shower

Little is more fun than a Polaroid at a party. Catch your guests being funny or sweet and create momentoes they will always cherish. Call local camera shops to see if you can rent a Polaroid. (Polaroid cameras produce the pictures right away. They're more expensive and the emulsion deteriorates more quickly, but they are fun in the moment.)

Do Yourself a Favor! Create Memories to Go

If you are the least bit crafts oriented, this will probably be your favorite part of the preparations. The best part is, you can do the favors tomorrow—they keep! That way, you'll be all set. First, how many do you make? I suggest you make five more than you think you'll need. What's the worst that can happen? You have some left over. I've provided at least one idea with each party theme for you to choose from.

Now, I've heard it said, "Grown women do not get or give party favors." Wrong! You want your guests to have a totally memorable time? Party favors say, "Thanks for participating" and give a pile of warm fuzzy feelings the next morning when she wakes up and sees it where she left it when she got home the night before!

So how do you do it? Well, I'm going to give you the easy way, because heck, some of you will get way more creative, and some of you will think even what I've suggested here is slave labor. Here are my easy steps to creating party favors.

First, answer this question yes or no:

I am armed with a glue gun and I know how to use one (without third-degree burns).

If you answered yes, you'll do great. If you answered no, you will learn with this project. Otherwise, try to get someone who's into this kind of thing to do this.

For the purpose of convenience, I am going to assume you have fifteen people coming to the shower, and you will therefore prepare twenty party favors.

Go to a crafts store. Look under "Party Supplies" in your Yellow Pages. They will have these adorable precut veil circles, about 6 inches in diameter, with ruffled (fluted) edges. Buy a package in pink, blue, and yellow.

Go to where they sell little plastic baby stuff. Like pacifiers, tiny cribs, plastic babies, stuff like that. They'll have a display of ideas right there for you to choose from. Steal their ideas, that's a good thing, or just do what I'm about to tell you.

Buy twenty pieces of some sort of plastic thing—let's say the little baby bottles. Buy a few sprays of wired beaded pearl sprays and some curling ribbon in the color(s) of the shower or pink, yellow, and blue.

Buy a glue gun and a package of glue sticks if you don't have them already.

(Better, cheaper, longer-lasting, serious glue guns are at the hardware store, but the silly pink ones at the crafts store will work just fine unless you plan to put in some serious hours with it in the future.)

Buy ¼ cup per guest of some kind of candy, like jelly beans or something else, or ½ cup per guest of some sort of potpourri.

OK, get out your glue gun, pinking shears, scissors, and a bowl. Dump the filling stuff (potpourri or candy) into the bowl. You're ready to go. Slap one piece of precut veil onto the middle of your clean work surface. Put ½ cup of potpourri or a handful of candy into the middle. Gather it up into a sachet/package or bundle. If

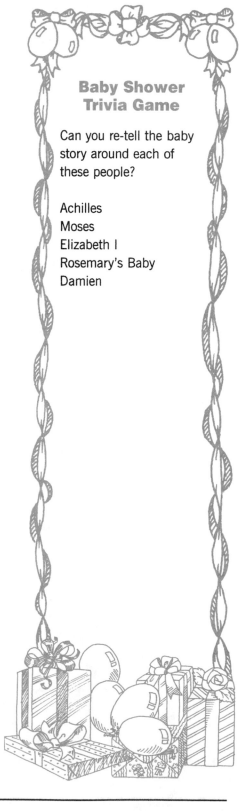

Baby Shower Trivia Game

Can you re-tell the baby story around each of these people?

Achilles
Moses
Elizabeth I
Rosemary's Baby
Damien

you are really worried about sealing it, use a small rubber band now, but it's not really necessary. (*Hint:* To make the potpourri sachets look plumper, put a cluster of five cotton balls or a tiny Styrofoam ball in the center before you seal the sachet!)

If you want your favor to hang, like a Christmas ornament, then take an 8-inch-long piece of ribbon and tie it tightly into a knot at one end. Hold it sideways, against the side of the sachet, and pull one end lengthwise through the other end. To secure the entire package, wrap another length of ribbon around it and double wrap it. Gather it up into a package and tie it tightly with a piece of ribbon. Tie it into a bow. Double knot the bow.

Now, take your plastic doo-dad and a pearl spray. With your hot glue gun, melt a drop of glue onto the very center of the bow. Count to five so the glue cools enough not to melt the cheap plastic doo-dad. Press in the pearl spray. Then press the plastic doo-dad firmly into the warm glue. Or, you could tie the doo-dad onto the ends/streamers of the ribbon. This will have to be your choice when you are assembling the projects. Voila! There you have it! That was easy, wasn't it? Stick all the favors in a long low box and you're done!

CHAPTER 12

Party Favors

Ideas for Party Goers

Some favors are indicated by the type of party you are having!
Consider these ideas, which are copied from Chapter 3. Something
here might spark an idea, even if it was originally intended for a
party with a different theme than yours!

- Plastic leis to wear
- Packages of food tied in Hawaiian fabric
- Fake sunglasses
- Boxed petit fours
- Filled, sealed plastic champagne glasses
- A decorated straw hat
- Something—small cornbreads? chili mix?— tied up in kerchiefs
- Little bottles of tanning lotion
- Sunglasses
- Bath tea sachets
- Little pots or baskets filled with tea bags
- Homemade candles
- A flower or topiary in a pot
- A cut flower tied with a ribbon
- A seed packet
- A tiny trowel with a bow
- Wooden spoons tied with ribbons or with the mother-to-be's name painted on them
- Spice holders made from yarn and cinnamon sticks
- A few sheets of writing paper and envelopes, wrapped nicely
- Little containers or bags filled with bath beads
- A discount coupon for a haircut or manicure
- Little alcohol bottles tied with ribbon
- Spools of white thread with a note tied with ribbon through the center that says "Thank you for coming"
- Coupons/tickets to a postbaby party you plan to hold
- Gift certificates to Blockbuster
- Bottles of CD cleaner with ribbons around their necks

- Those big dopey gauze hair bonnets our moms wore—or plastic rainbonnets
- Lace handkerchiefs
- Big floppy sun hats you decorated in advance and everyone wore at the party
- The project guests made at whatever art workshop you took them to (ceramics, stained glass, etc.)
- Lots of bubble gum
- A pair of bobby socks
- Little satin pillows
- Sleep masks
- A three-prong adapter you painted with fabric paint
- An extension cord
- A wreath of laurel leaves (silk or real)
- A brightly colored "Egyptian" armband made from electrician's wire
- Something else in keeping with the theme of the costumes for the shower—like quill pens if you did a patriotic shower
- A copy of a book that was featured or read from
- Admission to any class you provided, like a dance class of some type
- A brightly colored cardboard flower or peace sign
- A red gingham checked cloth napkin or two
- A candy pacifier on a string
- A bubble toy pacifier on a rope
- Boxed chocolates
- A tiny satin lingerie or jewelry case
- A quilted square
- A sampler of cheeses
- A bottle of wine
- A wine glass with the guest's name on it
- A shower cap
- A set of chopsticks
- A silk lipstick case

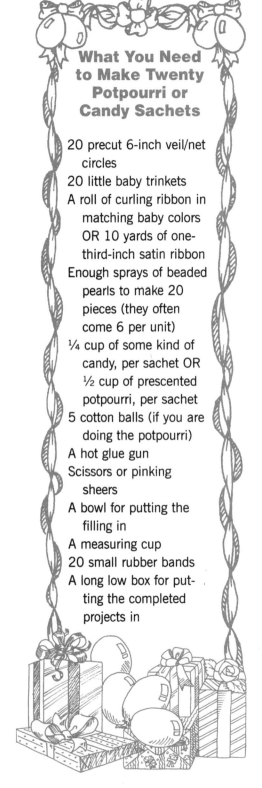

What You Need to Make Twenty Potpourri or Candy Sachets

20 precut 6-inch veil/net circles

20 little baby trinkets

A roll of curling ribbon in matching baby colors OR 10 yards of one-third-inch satin ribbon

Enough sprays of beaded pearls to make 20 pieces (they often come 6 per unit)

¼ cup of some kind of candy, per sachet OR ½ cup of prescented potpourri, per sachet

5 cotton balls (if you are doing the potpourri)

A hot glue gun

Scissors or pinking sheers

A bowl for putting the filling in

A measuring cup

20 small rubber bands

A long low box for putting the completed projects in

Party Favors You Can Create At Home

Baby Driving Swan

For each you'll need:

One mesh veil circle

¼ c. pink or blue jelly beans

One pink, blue, yellow, or white plastic swan

2 pearl sprays

⅓-inch wide ribbon to match the swan

A plastic baby (about 1½-inches tall)

Here's how to assemble:

Place the jelly beans in the circle and seal with ribbon. Stick the sachet of beans into the swan with a pearl spray skewered on both sides.

Wrap the baby in ribbon clothes by holding a piece along its back and wrapping over the shoulder, through the groin, around the other shoulder, around the other leg, and around its waist. Hot glue in place.

Take a short length of ribbon and glue one end to each of the baby's hands. Put the loop around the swan's neck as reins and put a drop of hot glue on the baby's bottom to keep it seated on the bag of jellybeans.

Decorated Booties

You can find cute plastic booties at the party goods store! For this favor you'll need:

1 hollow yellow baby bootie

1 chocolate teddy bear or pacifier candy

About 3 inches of gathered lace edging, no more than ¼-inch in diameter. Get the kind gathered on one side but seamed on the other.

About 3 inches of string pearls—the tiny plastic ones that come in pink, blue, yellow, and white in long thin ropes

A bit of matching ribbon

Here's how to assemble:

Using hot glue, apply the gathered lace to the top of the bootie, as if the baby were wearing decorated socks. Cover the seam/selvage of the lace with the string pearls.

Tie a bow with the ribbon and hot glue it onto the front of the bootie. Stick the pacifier or chocolate bear into the shoe. Easy!

Wicker or Plastic Carriages

At my craft store, they have tiny wicker baby carriages not more than 3 inches long. I've seen them also made of white plastic. Here's the idea. You'll need:

1 carriage
A bit of gathered ribbon not more than ⅓-inch wide
String pearls in pink, blue, white, or yellow
Very thin satin ribbon in one of the above colors
Cotton balls (maybe six)
Two small pieces of babyish fabric
A small plastic baby

Here's what to do:

Decorate the hood of the carriage by gluing first the lace, then the string pearls to the hood and around the edge of the carriage.

Make a small bow and glue it onto the center of the hood.

Cut the fabric so that it makes a blanket to cover the cotton balls you have placed in the bottom of the carriage. Cut another, slightly smaller, piece of fabric and fold it down like a blanket.

Stick the plastic baby in the carriage and glue the blankets and baby in snugly with a drop of glue on either side of the inside of the carriage.

Watch out! If you're using a glue gun on a plastic carriage, you will melt it if you touch it with the hot gun tip!

Baby Eggs

OK, this is a cute little idea I bet you never thought of. Here's what you'll need:

The Morning After . . . .

You were a perfect hostess. The party was flawless and your mother-to-be had a lovely time. There was enough good food for everyone, everyone seems to have had fun, she enjoyed herself thoroughly, and, truth be told, so did you.

You used paper plates and napkins; you remembered to put the leftovers into the fridge before you crashed last night. Now you crawl out of bed, slip into jeans, and wander into the kitchen (which is a disaster) for a cup of coffee. You sit down for half an hour, glancing calmly at the wreckage that is your home. You stretch your legs out, read a magazine, and wait. What are you waiting for? The doorbell to ring, of course! And when it does, you open the door to the one or two maids you hired from the local maid service. They

will have your place back to spotless in two hours, while you finish your magazine and take "Thank-you-I-had-a-great-time" calls from your mother-to-be and the guests.

Ah, life is perfect. You send a quiet good wish to this writer, saying, "Gee, Jennifer. You were right! It's much more important to have the house spotless after the party than it was the day of the party!" You muse how the simple truth I shared—that after five people get to your house, no one notices how dirty or clean it is—is a universal hosting truth.

When the maids leave at last, your house all tidy and fresh smelling, and you give them the check, you thank your lucky stars that you bought this book. Then you trot off to the mall.

1 egg per person attending
Red and blue food coloring
A yellow wax crayon
Tiny pink and blue satin ribbon
Hot glue gun
Snips of ruffled lace

Instructions:
1. With the yellow crayon, gently write in big letters on each egg "Brenda's Baby Shower." You can draw pictures if you want.
2. Get a large empty bowl and a fork.
3. Chip a tiny hole in one end of the raw egg. Holding it over the bowl, chip a tiny hole in the other end. Blow gently into one end of the hole so the egg's contents drain into the bowl. (You can use this for baking the shower cake, making a quiche or omelets, etc.) All you'll use from now on is the empty shell.
4. Run a tiny, slow stream of warm tap water through each egg to clean it thoroughly.
5. Just like Easter, place ten drops of food coloring, a pinch of salt, and some warm water in a bowl. Create one bowl of blue and one of pink/red.
6. Dip half the egg in the one color, half in the other. (The overlap will, of course, be purple!)
7. The yellow should be brightly illuminated on the now pink-and-blue egg.
8. Place back in carton to dry thoroughly, or on a wire baking rack.
9. When dry, take a 5-inch-long piece of ribbon and knot it at one end. Using a crochet hook, pull the loop through the egg so the knot in the ribbon can suspend it.
10. Seal the ends of the egg with a tiny circlet of lace.
11. Voila!

Baby Sachets
You'll need:
6 c. fragrant potpourri

12 plastic babies
Several yards of pregathered lace
Hot glue gun
Pink-and-blue ribbon
Cotton balls (a whole bag will be more than enough)
About 1 yard of gauze, lace, or organza

Instructions:

1. Fold fabric so that many 6-inch circles can be cut from it simultaneously. Using a 6-inch plastic container lid as a guide, cut twelve circles from the fabric.
2. Using the hot glue gun (or sewing machine), apply lace border to the perimeter of the right side of each circle.
3. Pour ½ c. of potpourri into the center of the wrong side of each circle.
4. Wad a clump of cotton balls to about handful size. (This gives it bulk.)
5. Place cotton balls in center. If you'd like, you can add a few drops of potpourri oil to each one.
6. Gather fabric circle around cotton and potpourri.
7. Tie closed with ribbon. Tie bows and hot glue babies in place.
8. Voila! Present in a large basket lined with a receiving blanket.

The Wilton Method

I was trained by Wilton to decorate cakes. If they have a competitor, I don't know about them. I am recommending them because I believe they are readily available around the country, and their stuff is good quality. In truth, if you can find something you like better, any brand will do.

You'll need:

1–2 trays of Wilton baby shower plastic molds (they come in small babies, cigars, unicorns, horses, roses, etc.) with stick spaces
Pink and blue Wilton candy melts
Candy flavoring (cherry, mint, chocolate, raspberry, etc.)

Supplier Resources

There are a number of excellent party goods places on the Web that will deliver just what you want, fast. The great thing about these kinds of places is in a half-hour with a computer, you can comparison shop, order everything you need, and be done with it. If you are having one of your teammates handle this part of the shower planning, make sure they get a copy of this list.

My favorite places for party goods include:

www.ShindigZ.com (all the party goods you can think of)

www.Partypro.com (more of all the party goods you can think of)

www.Oriental.com (everything you'd need for any of the themed parties in this book)

www.Currentcatalog.com (lots of paper goods at fair prices)

www.Babymagic.net (baby stuff)

www.Party411.com (party goods)

www.Bkpuffnstuff.com/baby.html (baby stuff)

www.Partythemes.com (great baby shower games)

www.Kandcpartycreations.com (baby shower stuff and ideas)

www.Eastsideweb.com (they will make special seed packets for your shower favors)

www.Epartysupply.com (discount supplies)

www.Weir.net/candy (specialty candy for your shower)

www.Maplesprings.com/baby.html (wonderful baby gifts)

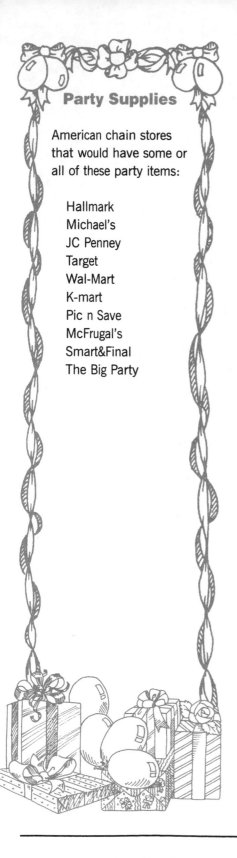

Party Supplies

American chain stores that would have some or all of these party items:

Hallmark
Michael's
JC Penney
Target
Wal-Mart
K-mart
Pic n Save
McFrugal's
Smart&Final
The Big Party

Lollipop wrappers
Lollipop sticks
Pink and/or blue baby ribbon (¼-inch wide)

Instructions:

1. This is too easy for words! All you have to do is wash the molds and dry them well.
2. Place a stick in the insert section on each mold.
3. Follow the directions on the candy molds package for adding flavor and for heating. DO NOT over microwave—they smell AWFUL when they burn and they'll not be useable. Really, the smell will keep guests, children, cockroaches, pets, and men out of your house for days, and it will kill your houseplants. Any guesses how I know this is almost true?
4. When the candy melts are properly liquid, pour them into the molds. I like to pour them half of pink, followed quickly by half of blue for baby showers. Tap the sides of the trays to release air bubbles.
5. Put in fridge to harden (about an hour or so).
6. Pop them from trays when hard by gently pressing with your thumb. If they don't pop right out of the molds, they aren't hard enough yet. Put in freezer for five minutes. Don't try to get them out by pulling the sticks only. You'll crack some of them.
7. Remove from trays and place in cellophane lolly bags. Tie necks with two colors of ribbon. How pretty!

CHAPTER 13

Worksheets

GUEST LIST WORKSHEET

NAME	ADDRESS	TELEPHONE	RSVP RECEIVED?
1.			
2.			
3.			
4.			
5.			
6.			
7.			
8.			
9.			
10.			
11.			
12.			
13.			
14.			
15.			
16.			
17.			
18.			
19.			
20.			
21.			
22.			
23.			
24.			
25.			

SHOWER GIFT RECORDER

NAME	DESCRIPTION OF GIFT	THANK-YOU NOTE SENT?

GIFT REGISTRY CHECKLIST

LARGE TICKET ITEMS	DESIRED QUANTITY:	QUANTITY RECEIVED:	MANUFACTURER:	PATTERN/MODEL:
Carriage/large stroller				
Umbrella stroller				
Crib				
Changing table				
Infant car seat				
Toddler car seat				
High chair				
Bouncing seat				
Portable play pen				
Bassinet				
Front personal baby carrier				
Rocking chair/glider				
Dresser				
Other:				

LAYETTE

	DESIRED QUANTITY:	QUANTITY RECEIVED:	MANUFACTURER:	PATTERN/MODEL:
Bassinet				
Crib sheets				
Crib skirt				
Crib comforter				
Crib blanket				
Swaddling blanket				
Cloth diapers				
Newborn nap shirt				
Undershirts				
Bunting				
Infant hat				
Sleepers				
Other:				

GENERAL CLOTHING

	DESIRED QUANTITY:	QUANTITY RECEIVED:	MANUFACTURER:	PATTERN/MODEL:
Outfits:				
Summer				
Fall				
Winter				
Spring				
Bibs				
Towels				
Washcloths				
Socks				
Mittens				

SITE WORKSHEET

Shower site:

Address:

Telephone:

Contact: Hours:

Appointments:

Date: Time:

Date: Time:

Date: Time:

Date: Time:

Cost:

Total amount due:

Amount of deposit: Date:

Balance due: Date:

Room reserved:

Date: Time: Number of hours:

Overtime cost:

Occupancy:

Final head count due date:

Location includes the following services:

Location includes the following equipment:

Terms of cancellation:

Other:

ITEM	DESCRIPTION	COST	NOTES
Shower Site			
Site rental			
Overtime fee			
Other			
Equipment			
Tent			
Chairs			
Tables			
Linens			
Other			
Service			
Servers			
Other (list below)			
TOTAL			

Caterer Worksheet

Name (if different from shower site):

Address:

Telephone:

Contact: Hours:

Appointments:

Date: Time:

Date: Time:

Date: Time:

Date of hired services: Time:

Number of hours: Cocktail hour:

Overtime cost: Final head count due date:

Menu:

Sit down or buffet?

Includes the following services:

Includes the following equipment:

Cost:

Total amount due:

Amount of deposit: Date:

Balance due: Date:

Gratuities included? ❑ Yes   ❑ No   Sales tax included?   ❑ Yes   ❑ No

Terms of cancellation:

Notes:

ITEM	DESCRIPTION	COST	NOTES
Food			
Appetizers			
Entrees			
Dessert			
Other food			
Beverages			
Nonalcoholic			
Champagne			
Wine			
Liquor			
Equipment			
Tent			
Chairs			
Tables			
Linens			
Dinnerware			
Flatware			
Glassware			
Serving pieces			
Other			
Service			
Servers			
Overtime cost			
Other			
Gratuities			
Sales tax			
TOTAL			

MENU AND BEVERAGE WORKSHEET

ITEM	DESCRIPTION	COST	NOTES
Appetizers			
Entrees			
Desserts (if any)			
Beverages (nonalcoholic)			
Wine			
Champagne			
Open bar			
Other			
Gratuities			
TOTAL			

REGISTRY WORKSHEET

Give a copy of this to any guests who may ask about possible gift ideas.

Name of store:

Locations:

Toll-free mail order number:

Name(s) registry listed under:

Notes:

Name of store:

Locations:

Toll-free mail order number:

Name(s) registry listed under:

Notes:

Name of store:

Locations:

Toll-free mail order number:

Name(s) registry listed under:

Notes:

INVITATION WORDING WORKSHEET

Sample Invitation #1

_____

_____

_____

_____

_____

_____

_____

_____

Sample Invitation #2

_____

_____

_____

_____

_____

_____

_____

_____

_____

SEATING DIAGRAM

List below which guests you would like to seat at each table:

Table 1	Table 2	Table 3	Table 4

Table 5	Table 6	Table 7	Table 8

Table 9	Table 10	Table 11	Table 12

Important Addresses and Telephone Numbers

Mother-to-Be:

Name: Address:

Telephone:

Father-to-Be:

Name: Address:

Telephone:

Family Members:

Name: Address:

Telephone:

Name: Address:

Telephone:

Name: Address:

Telephone:

Name: Address:

Telephone:

Party Committee Members:

Name: Address:

Telephone:

Name: Address:

Telephone:

Name: Address:

Telephone:

Name: Address:

Telephone:

Index

We Have

EVERYTHING!®

Available wherever books are sold!

Everything® **After College Book**
$12.95, 1-55850-847-3

Everything® **Astrology Book**
$12.95, 1-58062-062-0

Everything® **Baby Names Book**
$12.95, 1-55850-655-1

Everything® **Baby Shower Book**
$12.95, 1-58062-305-0

Everything® **Barbeque Cookbook**
$12.95, 1-58062-316-6

Everything® **Bartender's Book**
$9.95, 1-55850-536-9

Everything® **Bedtime Story Book**
$12.95, 1-58062-147-3

Everything® **Beer Book**
$12.95, 1-55850-843-0

Everything® **Bicycle Book**
$12.95, 1-55850-706-X

Everything® **Build Your Own Home Page**
$12.95, 1-58062-339-5

Everything® **Casino Gambling Book**
$12.95, 1-55850-762-0

Everything® **Cat Book**
$12.95, 1-55850-710-8

Everything® **Christmas Book**
$15.00, 1-55850-697-7

Everything® **College Survival Book**
$12.95, 1-55850-720-5

Everything® **Cover Letter Book**
$12.95, 1-58062-312-3

Everything® **Crossword and Puzzle Book**
$12.95, 1-55850-764-7

Everything® **Dating Book**
$12.95, 1-58062-185-6

Everything® **Dessert Book**
$12.95, 1-55850-717-5

Everything® **Dog Book**
$12.95, 1-58062-144-9

Everything® **Dreams Book**
$12.95, 1-55850-806-6

Everything® **Etiquette Book**
$12.95, 1-55850-807-4

Everything® **Family Tree Book**
$12.95, 1-55850-763-9

Everything® **Fly-Fishing Book**
$12.95, 1-58062-148-1

Everything® **Games Book**
$12.95, 1-55850-643-8

Everything® **Get-a-Job Book**
$12.95, 1-58062-223-2

The ultimate reference for couples planning their wedding!

- Scheduling, budgeting, etiquette, hiring caterers, florists, and photographers
- Ceremony & reception ideas
- Over 100 forms and checklists
- And much, much more!

$12.95, 384 pages, 8" x 9¼"

Personal finance made easy—and fun!

- Create a budget you can live with
- Manage your credit cards
- Set up investment plans
- Money-saving tax strategies
- And much, much more!

$12.95, 288 pages, 8" x 9¼"

Everything® **Get Published Book**
$12.95, 1-58062-315-8

Everything® **Get Ready For Baby Book**
$12.95, 1-55850-844-9

Everything® **Golf Book**
$12.95, 1-55850-814-7

Everything® **Guide to New York City**
$12.95, 1-58062-314-X

Everything® **Guide to Walt Disney World®,**
Universal Studios®, and
Greater Orlando
$12.95, 1-58062-404-9

Everything® **Guide to Washington D.C.**
$12.95, 1-58062-313-1

Everything® **Herbal Remedies Book**
$12.95, 1-58062-331-X

Everything® **Homeselling Book**
$12.95, 1-58062-304-2

Everything® **Homebuying Book**
$12.95, 1-58062-074-4

Everything® **Home Improvement Book**
$12.95, 1-55850-718-3

Everything® **Internet Book**
$12.95, 1-58062-073-6

Everything® **Investing Book**
$12.95, 1-58062-149-X

Everything® **Jewish Wedding Book**
$12.95, 1-55850-801-5

Everything® **Kids' Money Book**
$9.95, 1-58062-322-0

Everything® **Kids' Nature Book**
$9.95, 1-58062-321-2

Everything® **Kids' Puzzle Book**
$9.95, 1-58062-323-9

Everything® **Low-Fat High-Flavor**
Cookbook
$12.95, 1-55850-802-3

Everything® **Microsoft® Word 2000 Book**
$12.95, 1-58062-306-9

Everything® **Money Book**
$12.95, 1-58062-145-7

Everything® **One-Pot Cookbook**
$12.95, 1-58062-186-4

Everything® **Online Business Book**
$12.95, 1-58062-320-4

Everything® **Online Investing Book**
$12.95, 1-58062-338-7

Everything® **Pasta Book**
$12.95, 1-55850-719-1

Everything® **Pregnancy Book**
$12.95, 1-58062-146-5

Everything® **Pregnancy Organizer**
$15.00, 1-55850-336-0

Everything® **Resume Book**
$12.95, 1-58062-311-5

Everything® **Sailing Book**
$12.95, 1-58062-187-2

Everything® **Selling Book**
$12.95, 1-58062-319-0

Everything® **Study Book**
$12.95, 1-55850-615-2

Everything® **Tarot Book**
$12.95, 1-58062-191-0

Everything® **Toasts Book**
$12.95, 1-58062-189-9

Everything® **Total Fitness Book**
$12.95, 1-58062-318-2

Everything® **Trivia Book**
$12.95, 1-58062-143-0

Everything® **Tropical Fish Book**
$12.95, 1-58062-343-3

Everything® **Wedding Book, 2nd Edition**
$12.95, 1-58062-190-2

Everything® **Wedding Checklist**
$7.95, 1-55850-278-5

Everything® **Wedding Etiquette Book**
$7.95, 1-55850-550-4

Everything® **Wedding Organizer**
$15.00, 1-55850-828-7

Everything® **Wedding Shower Book**
$7.95, 1-58062-188-0

Everything® **Wedding Vows Book**
$7.95, 1-55850-364-1

Everything® **Wine Book**
$12.95, 1-55850-808-2

Everything® is a registered trademark
of Adams Media Corporation

$12.95, 304 pages, 8" x 9¼"

**Your friends and
family will be amazed
with what you can do!**

- Tutorials on the most
  popular programs
- Simple instructions to get
  your home page started
- Maintenance routines to
  keep your site fresh
- And much, much more!

$12.95, 320 pages, 8" x 9¼"

**A pregnancy book
that really does have
everything!**

- Extensive medical
  evaluation of what's
  happening to your body
- Exercise and diet tips
- 40-week pregnancy
  calendar
- And much, much more!

EVERYTHING **KIDS®**

Now Available!
Only $9.95 each

**For more information, or to order, call 800-872-5627
or visit www.adamsmedia.com/everything**
Adams Media Corporation, 260 Center Street, Holbrook, MA 02343